For Anna Rose, Jed, Isaac, Fifer, and Jenna

Interior design by Molly Heron
Photographs ©: AP/Wide World Photos: 115 (Mario Suriani), 97 (Leila Wynn), 83; Archive Photos: 82 (F-958/Express Newspapers), 44, 47 bottom, 81; Art Resource, NY: 6 (Fratelli Alinari), 7 (Werner Forman), 26 (Werner Forman Archive, Sir John Soane's Museum, London), 27 (Giraudon), 49 (Erich Lessing); Boltin Picture Library: 47 top; Corbis-Bettmann: 76, 94, 95 (Hulton-Deutsch Collection), 109 (UPI), 51, 64; Liaison Agency, Inc.: cover bottom inset (Patrick Aventurier), 22, 66, 75, 87, 92 (Hulton Getty), 61 (Peter Jordan); Mary Evans Picture Library: 29, 31, 39, 46; National Geographic Image Collection: 102, 112 (Kenneth Garrett), 62 (Hiram Bingham Collection); Photo Researchers, NY: cover top inset (Brian Brake), 116 (Chester Higgins Jr.), cover left (George Holton), 15 (Adam G. Sylvester); Stock Montage, Inc.: 45; Stone: cover right (David Hiser), 35 (Richard Passmore), 114 (Stuart Westmorland); The Art Archive: 17 (British Library), 8 (British Museum), 20, 23, 25.

Visit Franklin Watts on the Internet
at: http://publishing.grolier.com

Library of Congress Cataloging-in-Publication Data

Greenberg, Lorna.
    Digging into the past: pioneers of archeology/Lorna Greenberg and Margot F. Horwitz.
        p. cm.—(Lives in science)
    Includes bibliographical references (p.) and index.
    ISBN 0-531-11857-6
1.   Archaeologists—Biography—Juvenile   literature.   2.   Archaeology—History—Juvenile literature. [1. Archaeologists. 2. Archaeology.] I. Horwitz, Margot F. II. Title. III. Series.

CC110.G74 2001
930.1`092`2—dc21   00-033032

DIGGING
Into the
PAST

PIONEERS OF ARCHEOLOGY

LORNA GREENBERG and MARGOT F. HORWITZ

Lives in Science

FRANKLIN WATTS
A Division of Scholastic Inc.
New York • Toronto • London• Auckland • Sydney
Mexico City • New Delhi • Hong Kong
Danbury, Connecticut

CONTENTS

Chapter 1

INTRODUCTION: LOOKING INTO THE PAST

On the morning of August 24, A.D. 79 the long-smoldering Mount Vesuvius erupted violently—spewing lava, belching steam, shooting flames. For eighteen hours pumice showered down from the volcano's crater. Then there were several violent surges of gases and molten material. Each surge was followed by a flow of lava. The lava streamed down the mountain slopes to bury the small seaside resort of Herculaneum and a larger commercial center, Pompeii, two Roman settlements along the Bay of Naples in southern Italy. Buildings, streets, villas and smaller dwellings, vineyards, cemeteries, temples, theaters, fields, household vessels, shops, and even people were entombed—the heavy, scalding flow choking off the life of the cities. For centuries the sites remained deserted and uninhabited, and finally forgotten.

By chance, in 1732, a well digger uncovered a marble statue at Herculaneum and the ancient theater was discovered. Over the following decades, the sites of Herculaneum and Pompeii were excavated; first haphazardly by treasure seekers and then in a more careful way. The sites had been protected from destruction by human or natural forces for more than a millennium and a half by a thick layer of solidified mud and volcanic matter. Once recovered, they offered a preserved ancient world—a piece of the early Roman Empire—ready to be explored and studied. They offered a laboratory for the development of the science of archeology.

Archeology is a word created by the Greeks, from two words meaning "to study ancient things." It has come to mean the systematic study and interpretation of antiquities (objects from ancient times as a way to reconstruct human history from material remains—the artifacts or objects made by human beings. The traditional

These vases, pottery, and other objects were uncovered in Pompeii. In the early 1900s, archeologists agreed not to remove any treasures that they discovered at Pompeii. Instead, objects were kept where they were found and the city was preserved as it was after the eruption of Mount Vesuvius.

The ash that fell on Pompeii hardened to form a cast around objects. The bodies inside the casts disintegrated. In the 1860s, Guiseppi Fiorelli found a method to fill the casts with plaster to recreate the form of the person. When Vesuvius erupted, this man was probably driving a cart attached to a mule. He died with his back to a wall and his mule was found nearby.

spelling is archaeology, but the simpler form, archeology, is now widely used.

Archeology is rooted in human curiosity about the past: Who came before us? how did they live? How did we get to be the way we are? That curiosity is often stimulated by the mysterious monuments or structures we see around us that are not of our time: the pyramids, the Great Wall, Stonehenge, burial mounds, statues, ancient forts and walls, arrowheads that surface in a stream, stone or iron tools uncovered in the course of a construction project. Who walked down this path before us?

THE EARLIEST ARCHEOLOGISTS

History writers often try to designate the first person to sketch out a new field, and King Ashurbanipal of Assyria (668-627 B.C.), in the region of Mesopotamia, is sometimes called the first archeologist. He sent scribes to all parts of his empire to copy and translate any inscriptions they could find. He then created a library of 25,000 inscribed clay tablets, preserving the words of earlier generations. It is today an important resource for the study of Mesopotamian culture and history.

A century later, King Nabonidus, ruler of Babylon, was fascinated by the ruined temples and old inscriptions scattered through his empire. After excavating one monument, he left an inscribed clay cylinder: "The ziggurat is very old. I restored this ziggurat to its former

King Ashurbanipal is often called the first archeologist. This ancient carving shows a feast for the king. The king relaxes on a bed as food is brought to him.

The subject of archeology is the human past—a period of at least three million years, from the first appearance of humankind to the present. The study of cultures from a time before written records is called prehistoric archeology, or prehistory. For this period, archeology is the only source of knowledge. Archeology from the appearance of writing to the present is sometimes called text-aided archeology; both archeological and written sources are used. The people whose paintings have been found in the caves of France and Spain are known only through archeology. Our knowledge of Mesopotamia comes from both archeology and cuneiform inscriptions. Our knowledge of the Roman Empire derives from historical, written records, enriched by the finds of archeology.

state with mortar and baked bricks." A ziggurat is a pyramid-shaped tower of graduated levels. At a temple he proudly commemorated the finding of a foundation stone placed by Naram-Sin, ruler of Akkad, in the northern region of Mesopotamia, "which for 3,200 years no previous king had seen." (By modern techniques of dating, we now know he was overestimating the age of the stone by more than a thousand years). His daughter, Princess En-nigaldi-Nannar, also studied the past; she kept a collection of antiquities from southern Mesopotamia.

The scholars of ancient Greece were interested in their own ancestors, and in other civilizations and cultures, and speculated about earlier times. Hesiod (eighth century B.C.) wrote of the past heroic days of kings and warriors. The historian and traveler Herodotus (fifth century B.C.) wrote detailed accounts of people in other lands, and how they lived. The works of Homer tell of an earlier people. The Romans, too—Plato, Tacitus, Julius Caesar, and others—wrote of "the ancients." They wondered about earlier times but did not create a way to study them.

During the Middle Ages there was little interest in investigating the past. But in the sixteenth and seventeenth centuries, people again began to wonder about earlier times. Those of wealth and leisure traveled through Europe and the Mediterranean region; visiting monuments and collecting classical sculptures and other relics. A "Grand Tour" became an essential part of a fashionable person's education. The travelers brought home Greek and Roman antiquities to decorate their homes and gardens. A market for statues, jewelry, weapons, and paintings developed and soon dealers were sending agents out to scavenge through local markets and the countryside, buying, digging up, and stealing objects to sell. The hunger for artifacts led to treasure hunts, in which individuals, and sometimes troops of workers, smashed through ancient sites searching for items to please wealthy collectors. The sites—including Pompeii and Herculaneum—were looted and stripped of treasures. Collectors of more limited means went digging themselves—in their own backyards and local fields. In England and the Scandinavian regions many dug into ancient burial mounds and collected weapons, metal vessels, and human remains. Along with the treasures these collectors acquired or dug up, they were also enjoying the thrill of archeological discovery.

In the Americas, the first person we know of to actively conduct an archeological investigation was Thomas Jefferson. In 1784 he excavated a Native American mound near his plantation in Virginia. He was curious to learn who had built it, and who were the earlier residents of the area. He reported that it appeared to be a community burial site. He noted that the human bones were placed at different levels; in four strata, or layers, with earth and stones between them. He noted the placement of human bones and he cut through the mound to see its structure. In his summary, he estimated that more than a thousand bodies had been placed in the mound, many generations of people. Using instinct and his intelligence, this amateur conducted a scientific investigation into the past—decades before other excavators.

THE BEGINNINGS OF A SCIENCE

As the early treasure-hunters located ancient sites, they did great damage. At Herculaneum, in 1709, an Austrian prince sank shafts deep into the caked volcanic ash covering the city. Then, using gunpowder and force, his workers battered their way through the ruins, looking for bronze or marble sculptures, jewelry, coins, decorations—anything else that could be sold.

About twenty years later, Charles of Bourbon, King of the Two Sicilies, reopened the shafts under the watchful eyes of the Marchese Don Marcello Venuti, a scholar, an expert in antiquities. Venuti taught the workers how to avoid damaging the ruins. He recorded their findings and translated inscriptions. Later the site of Pompeii was also explored, at first by a hired band of convicts under instructions to dig for treasure; and then in the first large planned excavation in history, directed by a German-born art historian, J. J. Winckelmann. This is often called the beginning of the modern science of archeology. The purpose was not to acquire riches, but to investigate the remains of a past time.

The growing number of excavations, and of diggers, produced a jumble of artifacts, but little understanding of their meaning. In Scandinavia—a center of archeological activity—a Danish antiquary summed up the situation by saying that everything they had unearthed from earlier times was "wrapped in a thick fog." They could only guess at the age of an object, or which object was older or newer than the others were.

In 1816, a Danish National Museum was created from an antiquarian's collection), the curator, a former merchant, Christian Thomsen, devised a time sequence to use in arranging the museum's collections. It was called the "Three-Age System" and it used the materials from which prehistoric peoples had made their tools as a basis for a time scale. In the earliest period, the Stone Age, toolmakers used stone, wood, or bone. In the second age, the Bronze Age, they learned to make bronze (a metal alloy of copper and tin), and created their tools and weapons from that superior material. And, in the Iron Age, the more useful iron replaced bronze.

The Three-Age System was enormously useful. It provided a way to classify artifacts and to begin to understand the stages of human development. But Thomsen had developed it in his head; it was theoretical, with no supporting evidence. One of Thomsen's museum assistants, Jens Jaco Worsaae, then set out to test the idea by investigating in the field. By digging into burial mounds he found exactly what Thomsen had theorized: iron tools in the layers closest to the surface, bronze tools in the layers below; and stone tools in the lowest layers. In studying the layers, Worsaae was using stratigraphic observation—which became a basic principle of archeological excavation. Later scholars refined the Three-Age System, subdividing the Stone Age into Old (*Paleolithic*), Middle (*Mesolithic*), and New (*Neolithic*) periods.

A NEW WAY OF THINKING ABOUT THE PAST

One of the important results of the early researchers' work was the emergence of the idea that human beings had existed for a long time. Excavators uncovered human bones and artifacts at the same stratigraphic layers as extinct animals—hippopotamuses, mammoths, woolly rhinoceroses, and others. Through the study of rocks and soil, and the earth's crust, scientists saw that rocks had formed in layers, over the course of extremely long periods of time. By the mid-nineteenth century many scientists were questioning the accuracy of the formula set out by James Ussher, Archbishop of Armagh, in 1650, which stated that Creation took place at noon on October 23, 4004 B.C. Evidence was mounting that the world, and human life, was significantly older.

In 1859 the landmark book *On the Origin of Species by Means of Natural Selection* by Charles Darwin was published. The theory of evolution by natural selection provided a possible explanation for human biological change. Emboldened by a variety of reports of stone axes and extinct animals' bones located in the same ancient strata, a number of respected scientists announced their belief in the long history of human life. With these important developments, the science of archeology and the study of human prehistory and human evolution gained acceptance. Human history could now be explored. Archeologists would be the explorers.

DATING THE PAST

When the principle of stratigraphy was developed, archeologists had a way to establish "relative dating": older materials were found at lower levels of excavations.

A useful technique to provide "absolute dating" was dendrochronology, or tree-ring dating, which was developed in the early twentieth century. This was based on matching the patterns of rings living trees produce each year. Absolute dating allowed scientists to assign specific dates to artifacts and strata.

A major advance in absolute dating was the development of radiocarbon dating by an American chemist, Willard Libby, in the 1950s. He discovered that the age of organic materials could be determined by the amount of residual radioactive carbon they contain. (Radioactive carbon is present in all living things and decays at a steady rate after the organism dies.) Radiocarbon dating has been refined and is now a basic tool of archeology. Some newer techniques include uranium series dating, fission-track dating, thermoluminescence dating, and archaeomagnetic dating.

Chapter 2

"ONE OF THE GREATEST WONDERS OF THE WORLD"

GIOVANNI BELZONI ENTERS THE PYRAMID OF KHAFRE

For centuries, the great pyramid of King Khafre (Chefren) in Egypt had mystified all observers. The neighboring pyramid of Cheops had been entered, and the ruler's burial chamber found. But the second pyramid remained unconquered. Then, in 1818, the adventurer Giovanni Belzoni took on the challenge.

I seated myself in the shade. . . . My eyes were fixed on that enormous mass, which for so many ages has baffled . . . ancient and modern writers. Herodotus himself was deceived by the Egyptian priests, when told there were no chambers in it. The sight of the wonderful work before me astonished me as much, as the total obscurity in which we are of its origin, its interior, and its construction. In an intelligent age like the present, one of the greatest wonders of the world stood before us, without our knowing even whether it had any cavity in the interior, or if it were only one solid mass.

Knowing that it "seemed little short of madness to think of renewing the enterprise," Belzoni resolved to find a way to enter the pyramid—"without attempting we should never accomplish any-thing." After several days of observation and examination he ordered a crew of native workers to begin digging. Several disappointing weeks of false starts and dead ends followed, and Belzoni was becoming "an object of ridicule," and was called a "madman. " At last, in March 1818, his crew uncovered three large granite blocks, all inclining toward the center of the structure. They removed the stones and cleared a passage, then found a "fixed block of stone, which stared me in the face. . . putting an end to all my projects as I thought."

But Belzoni had practical knowledge of simple tools and engineering, and using levers and supports he managed to raise the stone. "I at last made the entrance large enough to squeeze myself in; and after thirty days exertion I had the pleasure of finding myself in the way to the central chamber of one of the two great pyramids of Egypt."

Belzoni was able to locate the entrance to the pyramid of Khafre.

When he entered that central chamber—he inscribed his name, G. B. Belzoni, in three-foot-high letters on the wall.

Among the early tomb robbers and adventurers, the most colorful and intriguing was Giovanni Battista Belzoni. Looking back, we can see that the methods he used were horrifying, but his achievements were astounding.

FROM PADUA TO ROME AND ENGLAND

Belzoni was such a unique figure that his life has been described by many—journalists, literary observers, historians, and later archeologists; but it is difficult to know which descriptions are accurate. We have his own account of his adventures, *Narrative of the Operations and Recent Discoveries within the Pyramids, Temples, Tombs, and Excavations, in Egypt and Nubia*, published in 1820, but he may have sometimes put a heroic slant on some details.

We do know—or at least are fairly certain—that he was born in Padua, in northern Italy, in November 1778, into the family of a struggling barber. He was the second of four sons. He made his way to Rome at about the age of sixteen. Stories of the next few years are confusing; some say he spent some time in a monastery: "I was preparing myself to become a monk," and he may have studied mechanical engineering for a period. He worked on the water pipes supplying Rome's famous fountains, gaining knowledge of "hydraulicks" he would later use creatively. (Hydraulics is the science of the motion of fluids; the purpose is usually to conduct water from one area to another, by canals or other means.) He then left Italy, traveling north over the Alps to Paris, and on to Holland, perhaps financing his travels by peddling religious articles.

Belzoni arrived in England in 1803. He was now an extraordinary looking young man—nearly seven feet (2.1m) tall (6' 7" by some accounts, but certainly very tall for his time), strong, and well-built. The writer Sir Walter Scott described him as "the handsomest man (for a giant) I ever saw." Richard Burton, an explorer, described him as "magnificent . . . strong as a Hercules, handsome as an Apollo." Indeed, he supported himself by working as a circus strongman and actor, performing at theaters and local fairs under a variety of titles including: the "Great Belzoni," "The Patagonian Samson," or "The Italian Giant." In an act as "The Young Hercules," Belzoni strutted before his audience, supporting five clinging men. When he appeared as the giant in "Jack, the Giant Killer," he dressed in a leopard-skin tunic and red boots, and walked around the stage carrying eleven or twelve other performers—sometimes with his new wife, Sarah, perched on top of the human pyramid. Charles Dickens later described her as "delicate-looking" and pretty, and Belzoni as an impoverished adventurer who became "one of the most illustrious men in Europe."

Belzoni used his knowledge of hydraulics to develop a "scientific" act called "A Most Curious Exhibition of Hydraulicks," which

Belzoni was a giant of a man who could easily lift more than half a dozen people. He appeared on stage as a strongman.

enthralled the audience with shooting fountains of fire and water. Belzoni later wrote, in the formal style of the period, that he supported himself for his nine years in England by his "own industry and the little knowledge I had acquired in various branches. I turned my chief attention to hydraulics, a science that I had learned in Rome. . . ."

BELZONI REACHES EGYPT

In 1813 Belzoni and his wife went to tour abroad; first in Spain, then Sicily and Malta. While in Malta, he met an agent of the new *khedive*, or governor of Egypt (Egypt was then under the control of Turkey)— Mohammed Ali, an Albanian soldier. Mohammed Ali wanted to modernize the country's traditional irrigation systems for farming and methods of flood control, and Belzoni saw this as his great opportunity. With his hydraulics and engineering background, he set out to design a waterwheel that—he claimed—would revolutionize agriculture in Egypt and restore life to the desert

In 1815 Belzoni, with his wife and a servant boy, James, arrived in Egypt, eager to present his plan to the governor. But the country was in the midst of an epidemic of plague and the travelers were immediately quarantined in a crowded hostel. Released after the epidemic eased, Belzoni faced another setback. Cairo was in turmoil, with conflict between the Egyptians and the ruling Turks, and mounting suspicion of the Europeans (called "Franks"), with their new and threatening ideas. As Belzoni was making his way on donkey to see the governor, a hostile Turkish solder attacked him and his leg was gashed. His audience with the governor was delayed for another month until he recovered. Finally, Belzoni had the chance to describe his waterwheel to Mohammed Ali, who was interested enough to ask Belzoni to build a prototype. After further difficulties obtaining supplies and help from uncooperative local laborers, Belzoni managed to construct his device: a large upright wooden treadmill that depended on the labor of just one ox. the traditional waterwheel (*saquiya*) required as many as four oxen.

A demonstration was scheduled, an ox was put in place, the machine was set to work, and the huge water wheel began to turn. It became clear that the invention was a success. Belzoni reported that "it could draw six or seven times as much water as the common machines. Then as a prank, James and a few native workers took the place of the ox. But as the machine gathered speed, the natives jumped off and James was thrown to the ground, breaking one or both legs (according to the source) as he landed. This accident was seen as a bad omen, and the governor—perhaps grateful for an excuse—abandoned the project. He knew that the people were opposed to Belzoni's invention, since it would require the labor of fewer animals and workers.

Stranded and needing money, Belzoni turned to the resources at hand. Like many other adventurers in Egypt, he decided to harvest the rich supply of antiquities buried in the sand. There were eager collectors, throughout Europe, ready to pay well for relics of ancient times. He had the skills for this new career: his knowledge of hydraulics and engineering, his circus-backstage experience in using levers and weights, his strength, his spirit of investigation and his real interest in the artifacts of the past, and his ability to charm. He met the British Consul-General in Egypt, Henry Salt. The British government had assigned Salt with the task of finding and acquiring antiquities to send back to England, to enrich the collection of the British Museum. The French government too had agents in Egypt, and the competition between the French and British treasure hunters was bitter and sometimes violent.

AN IMPOSSIBLE ASSIGNMENT

Salt was impressed by Belzoni's self-assurance and size, and his claim to engineering knowledge, and gave him a challenging—perhaps impossible—assignment. Belzoni was commissioned to move a huge statue of Ramesses II, a thirteenth century B.C. king, from Thebes to Alexandria. From there it was to be shipped to the British Museum.

The statue was actually a colossal granite head, three thousand years old, and weighing nearly eight tons. It lay half-buried in the sand at Thebes, on the west bank of the Nile, more than three hundred miles (480 km) from Cairo. It had been described as "the most beautiful and perfect piece of Egyptian sculpture." The French had made an effort to take it away, but found it too heavy to move.

Belzoni quickly set sail for Thebes. He described his entrance into the ruins: "It appeared to me like entering a city of giants, who, after a long conflict were all destroyed, leaving the ruins of their various temples as the only proofs of their former existence." He located the head "near the remains of its body and chair, with its face upwards, and apparently smiling on me at the thought of being taken to England." With local labor, Belzoni constructed a simple platform, using squared-off wooden beams made from tree trunks. The workers levered up the head with poles, first from one side and then the other, and pushed the platform beneath it. They tied the head on with ropes, raised the platform with levers, and inserted four tree trunks underneath to serve as rollers. Then the head could be pulled by ropes over the sand to the river.

Belzoni's drawing shows how he moved the huge head of Ramesses II.

Belzoni worked his men hard, as the annual flooding of the Nile was approaching. If they failed to get the statue to the river before that, the project would have to be put off for a year. He suffered through sunstroke, and dealt with an array of political and other problems and managed—in six weeks' time—to deliver the head to the banks of the Nile. Seventeen months later the head reached England and Belzoni was hailed as a national hero—responsible for bringing one of the largest pieces of Egyptian sculpture to the British Museum in London, where it is still on exhibit.

TREASURE HUNTING

By this time, Belzoni had read earlier travelers' and historians' accounts of Egypt, including the works of Herodotus, the Greek historian of the fifth century B.C., and had studied early maps, and used every chance to explore and visit the pyramids and other monuments. He was a ruthless looter, but he was also a careful observer and appreciated the grandeur of the ancient world. And his practical excavations would add a great deal to the knowledge and understanding of this world.

After his great success with the head of Ramesses II, Salt asked him to find and acquire more antiquities. Belzoni traveled through Egypt, searching for treasures for Salt, and for himself. On the Island of Philae, Belzoni saw a twenty-two-foot-high red granite obelisk (a four-sided, tapering stone pillar with a pyramidal top) lying on the ground, which, he thought, "if brought to England, might serve as a monument in some particular place or as an embellishment to the metropolis." He paid a local official to guard it until he could return to take it away. But when he came back, the removal was not simple. Just as his workers were about to load the obelisk onto a boat, the pier, "with the obelisk, and some of the men, took a slow movement, and majestically descended into the river." Belzoni managed to get the obelisk out of the water, using levers, and onto the boat. There were further problems, including a battle with a murderous band hired by a rival antiquities collector—but in time, the obelisk reached England.

By the end of 1816, Belzoni was ready for another adventure and proposed to Salt to "make another trip into Upper Egypt and Nubia, to open the temple at Ybsambul [Abu Simbel]." With Salt's agreement, he set off, now with a beard and wearing Turkish dress, which was cooler than his European clothes. He made stops along the way; particularly at Thebes, to search for mummies in the stone tombs of the Valley of Kings. Here the rulers of the Middle Kingdom (2040 to 1782 B.C.) were buried, in tombs cut deep into the cliffs. He battered his way into many of the tombs some of which had been plundered in ancient times but had not been entered since. He smashed doors, destroyed, and looted as

Belzoni adopted
Turkish-style clothing.

he searched for treasures—to sell, to keep in his own collection, and for the British Consul. He knew the dead were often buried with rolls of beautifully illustrated *papyri* (manuscripts written on papyrus reed paper) hidden in their wrappings, and with numerous small articles, grave goods, that he valued for their marketability, and as they showed "the domestic habits of the ancient Egyptians. " In his *Narrative*, he gives a colorful and horrifying picture of his efforts:

Of some of these tombs many persons could not withstand the suffocating air, which often causes fainting. A vast quantity of dust rises, so fine that it enters into the throat and nostrils, and chokes the nose and mouth to such a degree that it requires great power of lungs to resist it and the strong effluvia [flow of odors] of mummies. . . . In some places there is not more than a vacancy of a foot left, which you must contrive to pass through in a creeping posture like a snail, on pointed and keen stones, that cut like glass. After get-

After discovering the two temples at Abu Simbel, Belzoni made this drawing.

ting through these passages . . . you generally find a more commodious place, perhaps high enough to sit. But what a place of rest!—surrounded by bodies, by heaps of mummies in all directions. . . . I sought a resting place, found one and contrived to sit; but when my weight bore on the body of an Egyptian, it crushed it like a band-box. . . . I sunk altogether among the broken mummies, with a crash of bones, rags, and wooden cases. . . . every step I took I crushed a mummy in some part or other. . . . I proceeded from one cave to another, all full of mummies piled up in various ways, some standing, some lying, and some on their heads. The purpose of my researches was to rob the Egyptians of their papyri; of which I found a few hidden in their breasts, under their arms, in the space above the knees, or on the legs, and covered by numerous folds of cloth, that envelop the mummy.

BECOMING AN ARCHEOLOGIST

In July of 1817, Belzoni explored the site of Abu Simbel and cleared an entranceway through the sand to the twin carved rock temples built by Ramesses II. He then moved back to the Valley of Kings and began to search for overlooked tombs; using instinct and what he had learned from his observations. As he plundered, in competition with other plunderers, he was a careful, interested researcher. He took notes of everything he saw—wall paintings and reliefs, sculptures, architecture, pottery, and the embalmed people and animals. He measured, sketched, and copied, and he admired and learned. In one tomb, "the painted figures on the walls are so perfect, that they are the best adapted of any I ever saw to give a correct and clear idea of the Egyptian taste." At another, "We found a sarcophagus of granite, with two mummies in it, and in a corner a statue standing erect, six feet six inches (2 m) high, and beautifully cut out of sycamore-wood. . . ." From observation and experience, Belzoni was becoming an archeologist.

In the Valley of Kings he chose a likely spot to excavate:
I caused the earth to be opened at the foot of a steep hill, and under a torrent, which, when it rains, pours a very great quantity of water over the very spot I have caused to be dug. No one could imagine that the ancient

Egyptians would make the entrance . . . under a torrent of water; but I had strong reasons to suppose that there was a tomb in that place. . . .

A few days later the workers reached the entrance to a tomb, eighteen feet below the surface. After more digging, Belzoni could enter, and make his way along corridors, down steps, over a pit and into a square hall covered with paintings "so fine and perfect you would think they had been drawn only the day before," through more chambers into a vast hall with an arched roof decorated with signs of the zodiac. Amazed by what he saw in the center of the room, he wrote it "merits the most particular attention, not having its equal in the world. . . . a sarcophagus of the finest Oriental alabaster, nine feet five inches (2.9 m) long and three feet seven

In order to keep a record of what he discovered, Belzoni created a drawing of his observations inside the temple.

inches (1.1 m) wide. Its thickness is only two inches (50 mm); and it is transparent when a light is placed inside it. It is minutely sculptured within and without with several hundred figures. . . ."

Belzoni's spectacular find was the tomb of Seti I, the father of Ramesses II, who died about 1278 B.C. The sarcophagus was turned over to Salt, who sent it back to England and sold it to Sir John Soane, an architect and collector. It is now on view in the Soane Museum in London. Belzoni made wax impressions of the reliefs and hieroglyphics covering the walls in the tomb, including more than 180 nearly life-size figures, 800 smaller ones, and 500 inscriptions. He also hired an artist to make copies of the decorations. He planned to use these later to make a replica of the tomb so the public could view it.

Hieroglyphics carved on the lid of the sarcophagus of Seti I describe the journey of the sun through the twelve hours of the night. The text has been translated as saying that the boat of the sun-god enters the underworld.

THE SECOND PYRAMID

Belzoni now thought there was nothing more to find in the Valley and in 1818 moved to Giza, and the pyramids. He had visited them before and was fascinated by the second pyramid, which was generally thought to have no entrance.

Belzoni used his observation of other pyramids to calculate where the entrance might be and in less than three weeks he found it solving the centuries-old puzzle. Belzoni entered and managed to work his way down a narrow tunnel. At the end, after raising the block of granite, he squeezed into the heart of the structure; then followed passageways to what may have been the burial chamber of King Khafre, who built the monument as his tomb and place of eternal worship. Belzoni found the king's sarcophagus, but tomb robbers had entered 2,000 years earlier and it was empty. However, Belzoni's careful notes and measurements and descriptions of the interior formed an invaluable record for later archeologists.

After this great success, Belzoni discovered a black granite ten-foot (3m) statue of Amenhotep III. He had to turn it over to Salt, but, perhaps sorry to lose it, carved his name on the base. It is

Belzoni carved his name at the foot of this statue of Amenhotep III.

now in the British Museum, with Belzoni's name visible to all. Belzoni also made an expedition across the desert to the Red Sea port of Berenice.

MEMOIRS AND EXHIBITIONS, AND A LAST EXPEDITION

In 1819 Belzoni and his wife fled Egypt, after a number of attacks by rival treasure-seekers: "we embarked, thank God! for Europe," blaming the intolerable behavior of "some Europeans . . . whose conduct and mode of thinking are a disgrace to human nature." He was welcomed back in London as a celebrated traveler, and immediately began to write his memoirs, in English. They were based on his day-to-day diaries and were published in 1820, along with a volume of illustrations and an appendix: "Mrs. Belzoni's Trifling Account of the Women of Egypt, Nubia, and Syria." It was enjoyed by general readers and also appreciated by scholars for the mass of new information about life in ancient Egypt.

At the same time Belzoni worked to prepare an exhibit for the public. It was a full-scale plaster replica of the tomb of Seti I, made from his wax impressions, and shown with his collection of antiquities. It opened in London in May 1821 and was an enormous popular success.

By 1823 Belzoni was ready for another journey. He wanted to find the source of the River Niger and the fabled city of Timbuktu. However, soon after his arrival in Africa, he fell ill with dysentery and died, at the age of forty-five, on December 3, 1823. He was buried in what is now Nigeria.

Belzoni was surely a tomb-robber, and destroyed much in his search for treasures. But his observations and detailed notes showed an intense appreciation of history, and he played an important part in awakening an interest in the human past. His detailed accounts of his findings provided trail markings for the great Egyptologists who

Belzoni, the daring Italian explorer and archeologist, was often described as a distinguished-looking man.

Giovanni Belzoni

followed. A British journal, the *Quarterly Review,* wrote: "Though no scholar himself he may justly be considered as a pioneer of antiquarian researches." And Howard Carter, an archeologist who would later find the tomb of Tutankhamen, called Belzoni "one of the most remarkable men in the whole history of Egyptology."

Chapter 3
"SEEING WONDERFUL THINGS"

HOWARD CARTER AND LORD CARNARVON DISCOVER THE TOMB OF KING TUTANKHAMEN

After six unrewarding seasons of digging in Egypt's Valley of the Kings, money and patience were running out. For Howard Carter—pursuing his dream of finding the tomb of the "boy King," Tutankhamen, there was little time left. His patron and friend George Herbert, Lord Carnarvon, understood the need for slow and steady work, but it was clear that the project was a failure.

Pushing his workers for one last effort, in November of 1922, Carter ordered the re-excavation of some earlier work. He told his crew to dig deeper and wider. Within a few days, they came upon a sunken stairway, leading to a passage and then a sealed doorway. This, Carter was certain, was the entrance to the tomb. Determined that Carnarvon be present for the opening of the tomb, Carter waited a few days for his partner to join him in the Valley.

Finally standing with Carnarvon at the cleared doorway, Carter made a small hole in the upper part of the door. After widening the hole to insert a candle, Carter put his eye to the door and looked inside. He was struck dumb with amazement for a moment, which seemed like an eternity to his colleagues. When Carnarvon, unable to stand the suspense, asked if he could see anything, Carter uttered perhaps the most famous phrase in the history of archaeology: "yes, wonderful things!"

Howard Carter and George Herbert, Lord Carnarvon, could not have been more different men—in background, personality, and life expectations. But they are linked forever by the dramatic story of the discovery of the tomb of King Tutankhamen—one of archaeology's most significant explorations, a unique cooperative effort, which brought out the best in each man. An Egyptian pharaoh who lived

Howard Carter and his helpers inspect the sarcophagus of King Tut in the newly opened tomb.

only from about 1343 to 1325 B.C., Tutankhamen surrounded himself with objects of great beauty, which were discovered intact in his tomb during one of archeology's most extraordinary achievements.

Carter acknowledged his debt to Lord Carnarvon in the first words of the book he co-authored in 1923 with A. C. Mace, Assistant Keeper of the Department of Egyptian Antiquities at the Metropolitan Museum of Art, who was also a member of the expedition. In the book, *The Tomb of Tut*Ankh*Amen, Discovered by the Late Earl of Carnarvon and Howard Carter*, Carter noted that with the

> *full sympathy of my collaborator, Mr. Mace, I dedicate this account of the discovery of the tomb of Tut*ankh*Amen to the memory of my beloved friend and colleague, Lord Carnarvon, who died in the hour of his triumph. But for his untiring generosity and constant encouragement, our labours could never have been crowned with success. His judgment in ancient art has rarely been equalled. His efforts, which have done so much to extend our knowledge of Egyptology, will ever be honoured in history, and by me his memory will always be cherished.*

ART: A PATH OUT OF POVERTY

Were it not for their mutual interest in archeology, Howard Carter and Lord Carnarvon might never have met—so different were their early backgrounds and expectations.

Carter's grandfather was a gamekeeper on the Norfolk, England, estate of Lord Amherst of Hackney, a gentleman who took an interest in the people who worked for him, and in their children. When Carter's father showed a talent for animal painting, Lord Amherst financed his formal training. But because painters rarely had steady incomes, the eight Carter children grew up in difficult circumstances. They did not receive any education beyond the local village school, and their life prospects were dim.

But Howard, who was born in 1873, also showed an unusual artistic talent and trained himself for work in that field. Lord Amherst detected the young man's special skills and when Howard was seventeen years old introduced him to a distinguished Egyptologist P. E. Newberry. Newberry needed help with the process of inking tracings of scenes. (Actually, throughout his life, Carter was known as a fine draftsman—drawing plans and designs—and water colorist. At the age of fifty, in a "who's who" biography, he listed himself first as a painter, then an archeologist.)

His seventeenth year was a particularly important one for Howard Carter. After beginning his work with P. E. Newberry, he was hired out to Tell el Amarna in Egypt, to assist Flinders Petrie, a British Egyptologist who was co-founder of the modern method of excavation, which stressed the importance of all finds, large or small. Working for the first time in a real "dig" under a master archeologist who believed that every find should be meticulously catalogued, regardless of its significance, the young man realized that he had found his profession.

Carter had realized the importance of learning Arabic, and he became fluent in several dialects. This skill helped considerably when he was apprenticed to several eminent Egyptian archeologists. From the age of seventeen to twenty-three, he also worked with the illustrator Naville as a draftsman and illustrator at the excavation of the Temple of Queen Hatshepsut. Several years later, in 1900, Carter was appointed by Sir Gaston Maspero, Director of the Egyptian Antiquities Department, to an important post: Inspector-in-Charge of the monuments of Upper Egypt and Nubia, with headquarters in Thebes.

A city of ancient Egypt, Thebes flourished from the mid-twenty-second to the eighteenth century B.C., both as a royal residence and as the center for worship of the god Amun. It is northwest of the Valley of the Kings, where thirty of the greatest Egyptian kings had been buried, with ceremony appropriate to their unique civilization. They believed that for the mummy's well-being, it should be equipped to meet any later need, with much gold and treasure for the monarch's comfort and pleasure. It was also important that the tombs be secured against interference by placing mountains of stone over the burial site.

Carter spoke of the "romance" of the Valley of the Kings, remote

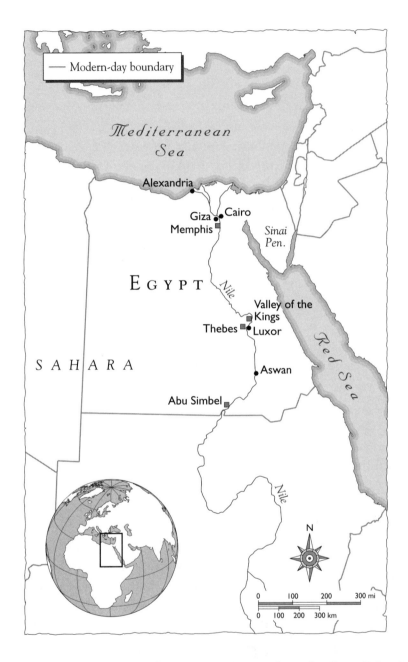

This map shows the location of many excavations performed in Egypt. Belzoni, Carter, and others explored in the Valley of the Kings.

from every sound of life, with the "Horn" the highest peak in the Theban hills, standing sentinel like a natural pyramid above the royal tombs—protection from those who would disturb the monarchs' eternal rest. But it was the very richness of their monuments which often proved the reason for the continual plundering of many of the tombs. Within a few generations, many mummies were disturbed and the treasures stolen, despite such protective devices as false passages, secret doorways, and mounds of heavy rock. Most tombs were broken into, with royal mummies being moved from place to place, in a desperate effort to keep them safe.

For the next three years, Carter did much clearing and restoration at Thebes, as well as at two other sites, Edfer and KomOmbo. Among the finds were the tombs of Tuthmosis IV of the Eighteenth Dynasty, and of Mentuhotep of the Eleventh Dynasty. Carter's tasks included

Massive seated statues of Ramesses II guard the entrance to the temple of Abu Simbel. Each statue is about 70 feet (21 m) high.

the installation of iron doors and electric lights for security against the plundering in the many tombs of the Valley of Kings, and also up river at the massive temples of Abu Simbel.

Carter was developing a varied range of skills. In addition to using his artistic ability, he was deepening his archeological knowledge for major jobs to come. His ability to speak Arabic helped in directing the Egyptian workers, and he was a thoroughly trained excavator. He had become knowledgeable about the unusual territory of the Valley of the Kings. Most important, he combined the craftsmanship of the artist with the practical skills of the engineer.

But all was not to continue to go smoothly. In 1903 Carter was transferred to the similar post of Inspector of the monuments of Lower and Middle Egypt, where his temper and strong will caused unnecessary problems. A group of drunken French tourists had been demanding admission to one of the important buildings after hours. One struck a guard, who reported the incident to Carter, the inspector, who told the guards to defend themselves. A fight followed, with the French getting the worst of it. The tourists complained to Carter's superior, who suggested that Carter apologize.

With the stubbornness that characterized his life, Carter refused to admit any wrongdoing, even a diplomatic one. He was then dismissed from the post, and retired to private life in Cairo. He lived precariously by painting and selling his watercolors for four years, before meeting Lord Carnarvon in 1907—an event that would lead to the discovery of King Tutankhamen's tomb and also create a relationship of mutual respect and affection that lasted until Carnarvon's death in 1923.

A CHARMED LIFE, DESPITE SADNESS

Only seven years separated Carter from his colleague, George Edward Stanhope Molyneux Herbert, known as Lord Porchester before he succeeded to his father's title of Carnarvon. But there was a world of difference between Carter's upbringing and that of "Porchy" in Highclere Castle, one of England's most stately homes.

The young heir, born in 1866, was one of four children of parents who treated everyone on the estate with kindness and consideration. As Porchester's sister Winifred Burghclere described their early lives, the "high-minded" parents treated the people of the village who worked for them as members of the family. Indeed, the little boy never heard or saw anything that "was common or mean."

Porchester lost his mother at the age of nine, but was raised with love by his devoted father and his two aunts, and the four siblings became very close. The young heir's education was somewhat progressive; unhappy at the confines of his school, he was able to study with a private tutor at home. Although quick to learn, he did not enjoy the classics which were so important to his scholarly father. When Porchester went off to prep school at Eton, many extra-curricular activities took precedence over his studies. As Lady Burghclere noted, "it is one of life's little ironies that a man destined to reveal a whole chapter of the ancient world to the twentieth century frankly detested the classics as they were taught at Eton."

With his father's agreement, Porchester left Eton early, to work with a tutor and to travel abroad. In 1885 he entered Trinity College, Cambridge, where he spent much time on sports. After leaving school, he sailed almost completely around the world, meeting with many adventures. He continued his habit, begun early, of collecting beautiful objects of art—from French prints and drawings to fine china and old books.

In the summer of 1890, on his father's death, Porchester became the fifth Earl of Carnarvon. He was twenty-three years old, and his fascination for travel continued; he was frequently off to Paris, Prague, Sweden, or Berlin. But when he married in 1895, he settled down to run the family lands and care for the employees who worked them. This was his family's traditional role for the earl.

Even when he settled down, Lord Carnarvon maintained his sense of adventure, and this trait inadvertently led to a life-altering accident. An early owner of an automobile, he was driving in Germany with his chauffeur in the passenger seat. They were traveling at high speed when they came to a sudden dip in the road. Swerving to miss some workers he could not have seen before, Lord Carnarvon caused the car to turn over, and he was pinned underneath before being rescued by his chauffeur and others nearby. He had major injuries—a severe concussion, burned legs, injured jaw and palate. Throughout the rest of his life, he suffered from a series of illnesses caused by these injuries, and he underwent many operations.

A CHANGE OF SCENE AND INTERESTS

Lord Carnarvon had to give up many of his activities because of the accident, but he took up another interest, archeology, which would make him famous. When his bad lungs forced him to leave England during the winter, to avoid bronchitis, he traveled to Egypt in 1903. Immediately he became fascinated by the world of excavation, and longed to make important discoveries. But he soon realized that he needed expert help if he were to discover any important ruins.

Consulting an Egyptologist, Sir Gaston Maspero, Carnarvon was advised to speak to Howard Carter. In the stubborn, yet intelligent and man daring, he found the expert he needed, and more—an explorer with imagination, a fine artist, and a person who would become a real friend. For the next sixteen years, the two men worked together—sometimes more successfully, sometimes less, but, as Carnarvon's sister wrote, they were "united not more by their common aim than by their mutual regard and affection."

Among their early projects together was an excavation at Deir el Bahari in Egypt in 1907. Writing to Lady Burghelere, the earl told of finding what they thought was an untouched tomb near the temple at Deir. After presenting one of the coffins in the tomb to a favorite museum in England, he found out that what they had thought was an untouched "tomb" was only a walled-up stable where the ancient Egyptian foreman had tethered his donkey and kept his accounts. "But this is a common occurrence," Carter wrote, "for in excavation it is generally the unexpected that happens and the unexpected is nearly always unpleasant." He realized that many tombs had been robbed in antiquity, and that it was rare to find one that was untouched.

Between 1907 and 1911, the men and their crews discovered many important tombs of nobles and working people. In 1914, Carter unearthed the long-sought tomb of King Amenhotep I of the Eighteenth Dynasty, followed the next year by the clearing of the interior of the tomb of Amenophis III of the same period.

Howard Carter tried to be of service to England during World War I as the King's Messenger, or official courier, in the Middle East. But again his quick temper and obstinacy caused his dismissal from office after a dispute over regulations. For his part, Lord Carnarvon was also anxious to join the war effort, and with his knowledge of French language and customs he would have been a valuable liaison officer. Unfortunately the physical problems resulting from this auto-mobile accident kept him from active participation. He had to be sat-

Lord Carnarvon supported Carter in his efforts to excavate the tomb of Tutankhamen.

isfied with the work he and Lady Carnarvon did in converting first their country estate, then their London home, into officers' hospitals.

Carter's interest in Tutankhamen had begun in 1908, after he read of Theodore Davis's excavations in the Valley of the Kings. While the tombs of all other great rulers of the Eighteenth and Nineteenth Dynasties in the Valley had been found (many by Carter himself), only Tutankhamen's remained left to trace. Carter was encouraged by the fact that no artifacts from the tomb had ever appeared on the market—a sign that grave robbers and other plunderers had not yet found these antiquities.

THE BOY KING

Tutankhamen had been a mysterious figure in Egyptian history from the time he ruled, approximately 1333 to 1325 B.C. He took over the throne while still a boy, during a period of political and religious controversy. (His predecessor, Akhenaten, had brought new religious cults into the kingdom, but Tutankhamen's officials worked to restore the ancient religion of the Sun God Amun, and returned the royal capital, which Akhenaten had moved, to Thebes.)

The boy king, as he has become known, was married to AnkhesenpaAten, Akhenaten's third daughter, making him an heir to the throne—a dangerous position at the time. The two were quite young—she may have been only ten years old—and there are charming paintings of the two playing in their garden. There were probably adults behind the throne, guiding the king in his actions and possibly planning their own power plays.

The actual cause of the king's death is unknown, although there are suggestions of death in battle or murder in the court. After Tutankhamen's death, his young widow attempted to continue her royal rule. She contacted the king of the Hittites, asking him to send one of his sons to become her king to provide the heirs she had not had with her first husband.

This request, however, did not reach the Hittite ruler for a long time, and in the meanwhile the Court Chamberlain, Ay, took over the throne. So Tutankhamen and his possible descendants disappeared from the scene. But while Tutankhamen ruled a short time, and was not well known as a king, his fame in death is remarkable: the discovery of his tomb is one of the most dramatic accomplishments in the field of archeology.

Carter's determination to find the tomb only increased after Davis's warning that there was "nothing left" in the Valley of the Kings. In the autumn of 1917 he started to work in earnest, and he labored for six seasons with no results. Lord Carnarvon, who had been granted the special permit required to excavate in the Valley, was becoming skeptical and appeared ready to call off the project.

A FINAL TRY THAT SUCCEEDED

Carter was certain that Tutankhamen's tomb was just waiting to be discovered. He convinced Lord Carnarvon to finance one more season, and returned to the Valley in the fall of 1922. His plan was to re-excavate the site of some preliminary work done in the first season, near the tomb of Ramesses VI. That work had yielded only the mud-brick foundations of some ancient workmen's huts.

By November 1, Carter had hired his workmen and was ready to begin. Their first task was to remove the workmen's huts, and clear away three feet of soil beneath the huts. Within several days, the group realized that they were at the entrance to a steep cut in the rock, a cut similar to those seen with of sunken stairways that often led to tombs. Two days later, their clearing of rubbish showed the distinct upper edges of a stairway, and further work led down sixteen steps to disclose a sealed doorway.

Carter could hardly contain his excitement. As he later wrote in his book, "Our years of patient labour were to be rewarded after all, and I think my first feeling was one of congratulation that my faith in the Valley had not been unjustified." Carter and his crew moved rapidly on, finding the royal seals which were evidence that the tomb had been built for a person of very high position. Equally important, the fact that the sealed door was entirely screened from above by the workmen's huts of the Twentieth Dynasty was clear proof that it had, at least from that date, not been entered.

Although anxious to get on with what he hoped would be the final effort before finding the tomb, Carter knew that Lord Carnarvon was in England, and must be contacted as soon as possible. He cabled the earl, "At last have made wonderful discovery in Valley, a magnificent tomb with seals intact; re-covered same for your arrival; congratulations."

Carter and his men then set to work to secure the doorway against interference. They had not worked all these years to leave the tomb vulnerable to plunderers. Carter also asked for the assistance of A. R. Callendar, an expert excavator who had worked for him years before. While waiting for Lord Carnarvon to arrive, Carter made the necessary preparations and purchases. Callendar and the crew removed the upper layer of rubble, to allow them to re-enter the staircase without delay. When they were all finally able to see the cleared doorway, the name of Tutankhamen was inscribed there, distinctly visible. On the night before the sealed doorway was to be removed, Mr. Engelbach, the Chief Inspector of the Egyptian Antiquities Department, visited the site to be part of the exciting event.

On November 25, the blocking of the door was removed and a descending passage was found. More rubble had to be cleared, but finally November 26 arrived: "the day of days, the most wonderful that I have ever lived through, and certainly one whose like I can never hope to see again," exulted Carter in his book.

The morning was occupied with the very careful moving of some delicate objects in the passage. But in the afternoon they came upon a second sealed doorway. "With trembling hands" Carter made a tiny hole in the upper left-hand corner of the doorway and inserted a candle. As his eyes became accustomed to the candle-lit area, details of the room slowly emerged. He saw gilt couches carved in the form of animals, life-sized statues of a king, painted and inlaid caskets, an inlaid throne. Everywhere there was the glint of gold.

Struck dumb by the vision, he stood and stared. But when Lord Carnarvon asked anxiously if he could see anything, Carter replied "Yes," adding, "wonderful things!" He immediately turned away and widened the hole further so that the two partners could see inside with a torch.

Howard Carter was not a well-educated man, but his description of the tomb is truly literary.

For the moment, time as a factor in human life has lost its meaning. Three thousand, four thousand years maybe have passed and gone since human feet last trod the floor on which you stand, and yet, as you note the signs of recent life around you-the half-filled bowl of mortar for the door, the blackened lamp, the finger-mark upon the freshly painted surface, the farewell garland dropped upon the threshold—you feel it might have been but yester-

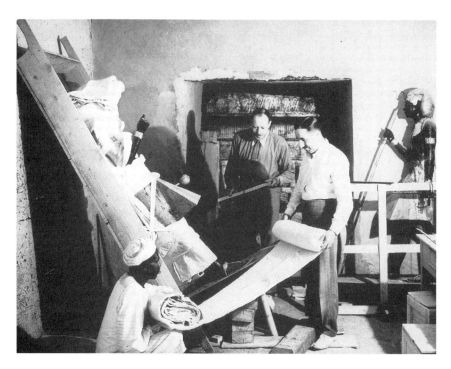

Carter and his assistant worked to remove objects from Tutankhamen's tomb.

day. The very air you breathe, unchanged throughout the centuries, you
share with those who laid the mummy to its rest. Time is annihilated by little
intimate details such as these, and you feel an intruder.

Carter and Carnarvon were "bewildered, overwhelmed" by the "museumful" of objects crowded into the little room. But they did not allow themselves to be overwhelmed for long. The men realized that they had to move carefully, that they needed a plan as well as a complete photographic record before anything was touched. It would be a painstaking process requiring skilled specialists during a time when little was known of conservation of artifacts.

Indeed, it would take two and a half months of painstaking work to clear the antechamber alone of its treasures. It was mid-February before the crew made its way carefully through more rubble to discover the immense gilt shrine built to cover and protect the sarcophagus. Working their way four feet down (1.2) from the antechamber, they came upon a magnificent gold and blue shrine beneath which was the burial chamber. It would take another three years before the king's coffin and its treasures would be ready to be removed from the burial chamber.

With news of the earlier discovery spreading rapidly, rumors abounded about the tomb and its riches. In an attempt to forestall gossip, Carter and Carnarvon held an official "opening" of the tomb on November 29, inviting Egyptian notables and officials a day later. But when the news reporter sent by *The Times* of London published his stories, the excitement caused tourists from around the world to flock to the site. Carter and his men were astonished, and the leader noted that "tourist visitors the Valley had always known, but heretofore it had been a business and not a garden party."

Tourism aside, there was much pressure on Carter to rush the findings, to show the world the marvels they had found. But he was not to be hurried, recording all of the objects from the tomb, and removing them one at a time, with painstaking thoroughness. Still, some critics called the crew "vandals" for moving the objects. Carter responded that by removing the antiquities to museums, "we are

For thousands of years, the boy king's mummified remains had securely rested inside his splendid sarcophagus.

really assuring their safety. Left in place they would inevitably become the prey of thieves and that, for all practical purposes, would be the end of them."

The Egyptian Museum in Cairo became the primary beneficiary of the treasures from the tomb, which filled most of the institution's second floor. A traveling exhibition of Tutankhamen's effects was one of the major art events of the late 1970s, a tour that included several cities in the United States as well as abroad. (Unfortunately, however, complete reports of the discovery in 1922 were not published, so later researchers have not been able to make full use of the findings.)

Within a month of the event, European and local press representatives were allowed to come to the site, along with local leaders from

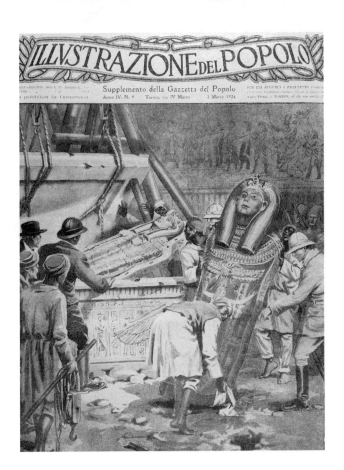

ILLVSTRAZIONE DEL POPOLO

Supplemento della Gazzetta del Popolo

Anno IV. N. 9   Torino, via IV Marzo   2 Marzo 1924

The cover of an Italian magazine showed Carter supervising the removal of treasures from the tomb.

Luxor who had been disappointed not to have been invited to the official opening. Shortly afterwards, sensational stories began to appear throughout the world, pandering to popular ignorance and superstition, about the "Curse of Tutankhamen." The curse was presumably on those who "disturbed his bones," and it was used to describe the early deaths of several people associated with the project.

The most attention-getting death was that of Lord Carnarvon. In poor health from the time of his accident, Lord Carnarvon was bitten by a mosquito on a visit to the Valley of the Kings in March of 1923. The bite became infected, and in those days before antibiotics, infection spread rapidly through his bloodstream. Pneumonia set in, and despite medical attempts, the earl died within three weeks.

Readers of the more sensational newspapers heard several bizarre

One of the treasures found in the king's tomb was this gold-covered wooden statue of the goddess Selket. The statue may have been placed there to guard his death chamber or to guide him on his journey into the underworld.

Here, Lord Carnarvon answers questions from reporters. Not long after the excavation of Tutankhamen's tomb, Lord Carnarvon was bitten by a mosquito, developed an infection, and died.

Found in the inner coffin, this huge death mask covered the head of Tutankhamen's mummy. It was made of gold and studded with precious stones.

stories about the "curse." The first tale was that at the very moment of Lord Carnarvon's death, all of the lights in Cairo went out and remained out for some time, as if to mark the passing of a great man. Another story centered on the little dog who had become Lord Carnarvon's faithful companion after his owner, the earl's son, went off to India. The fable relates that, also at the exact moment of the earl's death, the dog—at home in England—began to howl uncontrollably, and suddenly died.

Regardless of the stories, Carter and most of the people associated with him in the Tutankhamen project actually lived into their sixties, and several well beyond. For Carter, however, the sudden death of Lord Carnarvon was a personal tragedy. He wrote of the shadow across their lives, decrying the fact that Lord Carnarvon was not allowed to see the completion of the work.

"We, who are to carry it out, would dedicate to his memory, the best that in us lies."

Chapter 4
"A MARVELOUS LOST SANCTUARY FOUND"

HIRAM BINGHAM DISCOVERS MACHU PICCHU

*I*t had been a long, hard, and dangerous trek, and most members of Hiram Bingham's 1911 expedition in the Andes Mountains of Peru had no desire to leave the comfort of the hospitality they had found with two Indian farmers. But Bingham, their leader, sensed a special moment was at hand. He was certain they were on the edge of the discovery of the ruins of Machu Picchu, the secret capital of the Incas, which had been lost to civilization for three hundred years.

Guided by a small Indian boy, Bingham climbed up a ridge and rounded a point of land to suddenly see a group of ruined houses, built of the finest quality Inca stonework; then a mausoleum, and then an amazing structure—a Temple of the Sun. Building after building of the Incas' artful masonry, among the finest in the world, appeared. It took Bingham's breath away.

When he came upon a magnificent ceremonial structure, a masonry wall with three windows, Bingham realized he had indeed found the refuge of the remarkable Inca civilization. The discovery put the spectacular ruins on the archeological map, and insured Bingham's place among pioneers in the field.

Bingham's efforts to find the lost Inca capital stemmed from his fascination with the contributions of the Incas to civilization, which he believed had been ignored for thousands of years. The Inca people had built a great civilization in the highlands of Peru and Bolivia over several thousand years, beginning in the fifteenth century. The name Inca, which now refers to the entire culture, was originally used for the people's chief, a military and administrative genius named Pachacuti, who forged the scattered mountain peoples into a tightly organized society in 1438.

As Bingham wrote in the preface to his 1948 book, *Lost City of the Incas,* "Few Americans realize how much we owe to the ancient Peruvians. . . . They gave us the white potato, many varieties of Indian corn, and such useful drugs as quinine." Even more significantly,

This engraving was made in the eighteenth century. It shows the Incas worshipping the sun.

he noted, their civilization, "which took thousands of years to develop, was marked by inventive genius, artistic ability, and knowledge of agriculture which has never been surpassed."

But while the Inca rulers made sure that none of their millions of subjects were hungry or cold under their rule of total authority, they had no written language to record their history, not even hieroglyphics. To learn more about this unique people, Bingham turned to the historians of the sixteenth century, who looked at history and politics through a European perspective. He was determined to see, with his own eyes, the artifacts—what remained behind of a people who disappeared in the 1570s. This resolve led him to explore an area of the Andes Mountains far off the traveled route followed by most explorers.

AN EXOTIC CHILDHOOD

Hiram Bingham's sense of adventure was instilled by his grandfather, Hiram Bingham I, a courageous, hardheaded New Englander who became a Calvinist minister in the remote South Sea Islands. His first post was a mission in Samoa, before he settled in the Hawaiian Islands, where he preached his first sermon in 1820. Building the first Christian church on the island of Oahu, the minister also wrote the first Hawaiian-English dictionary.

Carrying on his father's missionary work on Oahu, Hiram Bingham II also enlarged the parish and translated the Bible into Hawaiian. This unusual home life, which taught strong Christian values in an exotic setting, was the setting for Hiram III's childhood. Born in 1875 in the Hawaiian Islands, he was given an early New England education with solid Calvinist ideals, including respect for people of other races, their manners and customs, and their way of life.

Hiram's father also instilled in him a sense of curiosity, an interest in searching for unknown facts, as well as a love of the outdoors. Hiram II taught the boy mountain climbing from the time he was four years of age. Indeed, the son developed a lifelong passion for reaching the top of the mountain and surveying the unexplored lands below.

After completing his early education in the Hawaiian Islands, Hiram followed the family's New England tradition and went to the United States to study at Phillips Academy and Andover preparatory schools before entering Yale University. At Yale, the sociable young man combined an enthusiasm for clubs and outdoor life with an interest in religion. After graduation, he returned to Oahu for a short time, serving as pastor of the Panama Chapel in Honolulu. At this point, he moved into business and became a land surveyor for the American Sugar Company.

FINDING AN EDUCATIONAL FOCUS

Realizing that he needed more education, Hiram used the money saved from his jobs and studied for an M.A. degree in history and social science at the University of California at Berkeley. He became aware of the lack of information on South American history, and began to see himself as a pioneer researcher in the field. Bingham went on to Harvard University, where he became a graduate instructor and received M.A. and Ph.D. degrees in history in 1905.

Bingham was invited to teach at Princeton University by then dean (and later United States president) Woodrow Wilson. While he enjoyed teaching, it did not appeal to him as much as field research. Because he was fascinated by the three-hundred-year period of Spanish domination in South America, he decided that his first trip to that continent, in 1906, would follow the 1819 route of Simon Bolivar, the South American liberator.

Traveling on horseback, by carriage, and on foot through Venezuela and Colombia, Bingham traced the route Bolivar's rag-tag army of British and Irish Volunteers and Venezuelan patriots had taken as they moved through tropical plains and swamps. He followed their path over the freezing passes of the Andes mountains, to the point where the rebels met and defeated a royalist army, breaking Spain's oppressive hold on South America by liberating Peru and present-day Bolivia 1823-24. (Bolivar later became president of

Greater Colombia—now Colombia, Venezuela, and Ecuador.) It was this remarkable journey which stayed in Bingham's mind, ready to be used later, when the explorer set off on his own historic adventure.

After he published his report on Bolivar's triumph, Bingham returned to Yale to become curator of South American history for the university's library. With enthusiasm, he helped build the library's Latin American collection into one of the finest in the United States. But Bingham was not to stay long in university library work; in fact, his first South American adventure had planted an idea of a dramatic journey of exploration and discovery.

A PRESIDENTIAL APPOINTMENT

The paper that Bingham published on Simon Bolivar received more attention than the young man could have anticipated. One person who read it with great interest was Elihu Root, President Theodore Roosevelt's Secretary of State, who had a strong interest in Latin America. After hearing of Root's enthusiasm for the young man's work, the president invited Bingham to attend the first Pan-American Scientific Conference in Santiago, Chile, in 1909, and appointed Bingham a Yale University delegate and a representative of the United States government.

Seizing the opportunity for an adventure, Bingham left early for the conference. Instead of sailing directly to Chile, he and his college friend Huntington Smith decided to follow the old Spanish trade route, the historic colonial highway in South America that linked Buenos Aires in Argentina to Potosi and Lima in Peru. The road had first been built by the ancient Incas, and then used by their cruel conqueror, Francisco Pizarro, in the early sixteenth century—as well as by Spanish viceroys, silver mine operators, and other seekers of fortune.

Bingham and Smith sailed from New York in September 1908, traveling first to London, where scheduled steamers left weekly for South America. The rest of their journey was by horseback, railroad and steamer. After their trek, they finally arrived in Chile for the two-week conference. There they met South America's leading intellectuals, including Peruvian historian Don Carlos Romero, who suggested that they visit the Inca ruins near Lake Titicaca and those at Cuzco, in Peru. Remembering Elihu Root's instruction that as a goodwill ambassador he should follow the wishes of his South American hosts, Bingham put aside his desire to return home. He also decided to bring along on the excursion his Yale classmate, Clarence Hay, who happened to be traveling in South America.

Bingham and Hay met in Peru, beginning a trip that amazed them with the beauty of the Inca ruins—ancient palaces, temples, and the houses of the Virgins of the Sun—and the impressive engineering skills of this ancient people. With tools no harder than bronze, no powerful work animals, and no wheeled vehicles, the Incas were able to move huge rocks into place. These and other remarkable feats would greet Bingham and his party a few years later, when they finally found Machu Picchu.

Although excited by the ruins, Bingham was still ready to go home. But before his departure from Peru, he was visited by the chief official prefect of the province of Apurimac, Don Jose J. Nunez. The prefect invited him to explore the Inca ruins of Choqquequirau, to "report their importance to the President of Peru." Nunez told them that these ruins were believed to be the secret retreat of the last Inca emperors after the Spanish conquerors overthrew their empire. Bingham tried to explain politely that he was ready to leave Peru, but Nunez was insistent, even when Bingham tried to explain that he did not consider himself an archeologist. Finally, with Secretary Root's instructions on diplomacy in mind, he agreed to put off his trip home once again.

There was no question that this was the worst possible time to visit the Inca ruins—it was February, the height of the rainy season. Worse, it was the rainiest month of the rainiest season in twenty-five years. But Bingham decided that it was important to go. As it turned out, "without Nunez and his practical interest in Choqquequirau, I shouldn't have been tempted to look for the Inca ruins and find two cities lost to geographical knowledge for several centuries."

Through his earlier studies of documents of the Spanish conquerors, Bingham knew that the Incas had reached a high level of civilization and had created the greatest empire in the Americas. He also knew that they had a long and difficult struggle to survive against the Spanish conquerors, which ended in their destruction in the 1530s by the tough, illiterate soldier Francisco Pizzaro.

Bingham feared that his trip would not be an easy one, and he was right. He and his handful of fellow explorers, including Clarence Hay, faced many hardships, including rock slides and the aftermath of an avalanche which had obliterated part of the route. The remaining trail was precipitous and icy, and the Apurimac River below churned like an ocean in a hurricane. The party had to cross a long, narrow bridge on their hands and knees, trying not to notice how it swayed above the angry water. After they crossed the river they had to climb hundreds of feet, in the very thin air at that high altitude.

Finally they reached the top of the canyon—Choqquequirau—twelve thousand feet (3636) above the river. The ruins consisted of three different groups of buildings, surrounded by terraces for defense. Following directions in a guidebook published by the British Royal Geographic Society, Bingham and Hay took careful measurements of the ruins of the most important buildings, made a rough map of the site, and took many photographs. They spent several days digging shafts and test trenches, trying without much success to find artifacts of the Inca people. They uncovered only some remnants of fabric looms, pottery, skeletons, and human skulls.

With his background in history, Bingham used historical documents as a starting point in his archeological work (as when he followed Bolivar's path). He became convinced that this site had been a fortress, not the last home of the Inca emperors. It had been built to protect the old Inca capital, Cuzco, from the aggressive Indians who came up the valley from the Amazon River. Although Bingham and some other members of the party were disappointed not to find the lost city, the leader's imagination was stirred. If Choqquequirau was not that last city of the Incas, what was? There was a forty-year period when they lived somewhere after being driven from Cuzco by the Spaniards in the 1530s, but where? He was now determined to find out.

When Bingham paid his respects to Peruvian president Leguia after the trip to Choqquequirau, the explorer consulted with Don Carlos Romero, the nation's leading historian. The two scholars realized that they were in the minority—most historians believed that Choqquequirau was the last stronghold of the Incas. Romero showed Bingham some old Spanish documents recording the last days of the Inca leaders, and Bingham looked through more writings, by historians of the Spanish and Inca periods. For the moment, however, the search was halted. After being away more than six months, he wanted to get home to his family.

RETURNING HOME—BUT NOT FOR LONG

Although Bingham continued to be intrigued by the mystery of the Incas, he returned to Yale where he immediately plunged back into his family and professional life. For a time he did not focus on returning to Peru. But during the summer of 1910, while working on the final drafts of his book, *Across South America*, he asked a friend, Edward Harkness, to read the proofs of the book. Intrigued, Harkness suggested that it might be the right time for an expedition to find the Incas—and that he would pay the expenses of sending a geologist along with Bingham to study the structure of the ground.

The idea fascinated Bingham. Actually, during the period when he was working on his book and on reports on the Pan American conference, he had found time at night to go through the documents and histories about the Incas, putting together clues like a detective on the leaders and lands he found so compelling.

Bingham began to envision a real scientific expedition—not just a trip. He would go through a cross-section of Peru, searching for the mysterious Mount Coropuna which he had read about but could not find on any map, and also cross through the ancient Inca strongholds in the heart of the Andes Mountains. He would carefully map the region, and collect specimens of animals and plants, while searching for the Inca ruins. He decided to invite specialists in several areas: an anthropologist-archeologist to study the ruins and the people in the region, a naturalist, a geologist, a topographer-mapmaker, and a historian.

A major consideration was timing: when would be the best season to start? The months of June and July made sense, because the rainfall would be light. He would start the group working in the high country, then move toward the coast in November as the Peruvian summer set in, to survey the mysterious Mount Coropuna.

PLANS FALL INTO PLACE

One serious problem remained: money. How could he fund the passage, expenses, and salaries of the five or six people needed in addition to Harkness's geologist and himself? A college classmate had the answer: plan to make it a Yale expedition! With the University's approval, he could ask them to offer two scientists a paid leave of absence and he could write to classmates for contributions.

Others were intrigued by the expedition. President Taft agreed to a loan of government topographic and surveying equipment, and George Eastman, of the Kodak company, gave each expedition member a camera, field development kits, and all necessary film (a good test for his company's new products, Eastman believed). By the spring of 1911, the group was set, with Dr. William Gage Erving added as expedition surgeon.

While the doctor and one of the civil engineers left in May, Bingham and the main part of the group sailed on June 8 for Cuzco. Here, as they made final preparations, they met a native prospector who described the ruins on the mountain calledMachu Picchu and the smaller mountain, Huaynu Picchu, as "much finer" than those at Choqquequirau. As the expedition got underway in July, Hiram Bingham kept the old man's words in mind.

Shortly after the expedition began, the group had an interesting experience. While traveling through a variety of different terrain

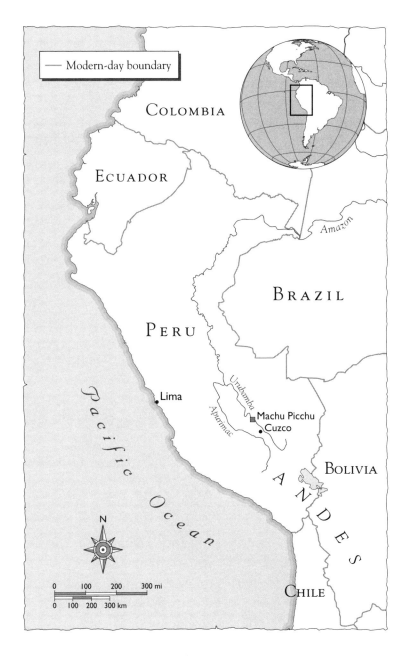

This map shows where Bingham and his assistants discovered Machu Picchu high in the Andes Mountains.

beyond Cuzco, they came upon the gateway of the Grand Canyon of the Urubamba River. They decided to camp for the night, but refused to stay at a dirty thatch hut along the road which served as an "inn" for travelers. The hut's owner was angry at their slight to his "hospitality," but commented that there were good Inca ruins across the river. He said that these ruins were on top of the mountains called Huaynu Picchu and Machu Picchu. For a price, he would lead them there.

THE LOST CITY, FOUND AT LAST

Sensing that they could be nearing their destination, Bingham agreed to pay the guide's going-rate—fifty cents a day for a "difficult" trail. The next day—July 24—dawned rainy and cold, and Bingham had difficulty getting a party together to climb the eight-to nine-thousand foot (2424-to-2727m) high Machu Picchu. The guide, Arteaga, was also hesitant because of the weather, but the promise of more money, a Peruvian sol, or silver dollar, persuaded him to lead the handful of men willing to make the trip.

The excursion was difficult in every way. They had to move on their hands and knees to maneuver on a primitive bridge over the rapids of the Urubamba River, then make a steep, hard climb hampered by excessive heat and humidity. The group had a brief but pleasant respite when they found a grass hut with two kind Indians who offered them water and baked sweet potatoes, as well as advice on the ruins that lay ahead.

The guide Arteaga mentioned to the explorers that the Indians and a young boy had apparently lived on this mountain shoulder with the magnificent views for four years, happy to farm small terraces of land and live far from other people. Finally, Bingham decided it was time to move on. With the young boy now his guide, he was led around the mountain bluff, where he found a series of ancient terraces, then a heavily wooded section.

The most dramatic discovery was just ahead. Suddenly, Bingham saw the walls of ruined buildings that had been constructed with great skill, then a cave of more finely cut stone. Above the cave was a semicircular building connected to another wall of carefully matched blocks of pure white granite. Bingham could hardly believe his eyes—the workmanship was as fine as in any Greek temple.

More and more buildings now came into view, with a stairway of granite blocks and a block that must have been an altar, or possibly a throne for the priests. An even more striking building was across the courtyard, with a massive stone wall framing three great windows that

Bingham found the ruins of Machu Picchu carved into a mountain ridge high in the Andes.

looked out over the canyon below. Knowing that because of the cold, thin mountain air people would be unlikely to have windows in most buildings, Bingham had the thought that it must be a temple, with a ceremonial purpose.

He could not believe the grace and delicacy of the work; he sensed again the special nature of the stonework of the wall and its adjoining semi-circular temple over the cave. Thinking back to his Inca history readings, Bingham remembered that a remarkable Inca ruler, Manco the Great, had ordered works to be made at his birth-place of a masonry wall with three windows. It was possible that this

Bingham sits on an Inca shrine carved out of a rock formation.

could be the capital of the last Inca people, who had a great civilization before being dispersed and crushed in 1572.

After the discovery of these special ruins, Bingham and his colleagues spent as much time as they could making sketches and cataloguing their findings. By the end of 1911, as the rainy season arrived, it was time to leave the ruins and return to the United States. But Bingham was not satisfied, and decided that he had to return to Peru. The results of the 1911 expedition were so impressive that Yale provided ten thousand dollars and the National Geographic Society another ten thousand, for further exploration.

Bingham was in charge of an expedition in 1912, as well as two even larger expeditions in 1914 and 1915. The 1912 project cleared and restored the site at Machu Picchu with the full support of the Peruvian government and the Prefecture of Cuzco, while the later groups found more Inca artifacts, including more homes. But after these successful seasons of explorations, Bingham was forced to flee Peru for violating excavation permit laws. He never returned for further exploration.

BECOMING A PILOT AND A POLITICIAN

Having lost none of his sense of adventure, Hiram Bingham determined to become a flyer—at the age of forty-two—to help the United States as the country prepared to enter World War I. Though flying was extremely dangerous at that time, he flew many missions for the Army, before being transferred to Washington, D.C., to help set up training programs for pilots. He also took command of the largest American military training school in Europe.

After World War I, he was elected Connecticut's lieutenant governor in 1922 and then elected governor in 1924. Before he could be inaugurated, one of Connecticut's senators died. Bingham then ran for the post in a special election and won—the only man in American history to serve as lieutenant governor, governor, and senator within twelve hours. He was elected to a full term in the Senate, where he served under Presidents Coolidge and Hoover. After his

Bingham served as lieutenant governor and U.S. senator for the state of Connecticut.

Senate career, Bingham stayed in politics, serving under President Harry Truman as chief of the Loyalty Review Board.

Hiram Bingham died in 1956, at the age of eighty. He had an almost unbelievable life, from exploring to flying to politics. But he may best be remembered for putting the spectacular ruins high in the Andes Mountains on the archeological map. He charmed the world with his account of the astounding fortress called Machu Picchu, named for its mountain site northwest of the Inca capital of Cuzco.

Chapter 5
"THE GLORY THAT IS INDIA"

MORTIMER WHEELER EXPLORES
THE INDUS VALLEY CIVILIZATION

With the outbreak of World War II, Mortimer Wheeler, a British archeologist, set aside his flourishing career to volunteer in the British Army. In July 1943, he was stationed in Algiers, North Africa, when he received what he described in a letter as a bombshell: "The other day I was returning to my tent in the evening sun when my Corps Commander dashed along with a [radio message] . . . and the remark—'I say, have you seen this—they want you as Director General of Archaeology in India.'"

By the next February, Wheeler was sailing in a slow-moving ship convoy, through the Mediterranean and the Suez Canal, on the long voyage to Bombay. There he would take up this "impossible assignment" in a country he had never even visited: to manage an archeological kingdom that sprawled over one and a half million square miles (3,900,000 sq km), with thousands of monuments ranging from simple shaped stones to the beautiful Taj Mahal, seven museums, a large, dispirited staff, and many vast, only partially explored sites throughout the region. When he left, four years later, he had accomplished wonders, bringing to light an extraordinary early civilization that had been little known or understood before his arrival.

A MODERN ARCHEOLOGIST

In the twentieth century, archeology developed from an adventure into a science, and the treasure hunters of earlier times were gradually replaced by professionals, with scientific backgrounds and thorough training. One of the most important leaders of this change was Mortimer Wheeler, a British archeologist who—while as extraordinary a person as the daring figures who preceded him—was a determined, demanding professional. He bridged the two periods and was the first truly modern excavator, bringing the use of thorough organization, careful techniques, and scientific methods to archeological discovery.

Sir Mortimer Wheeler holds some archeological discoveries from the London Museum.

EARLY EXPERIENCES

Mortimer Wheeler's first memory, as he later described it, is of himself at age three, trotting behind his father, across the Braid Hills of Edinburgh, and piping along with his father's rendition of the song of the Scottish lark: "To-wit to-wee, to-wit to-wee." Through the whole of his long life, Wheeler kept this ability: to hold in his mind an image—he called it a pictorial reflex—that carried all the information and the emotion of an event or a moment in his life.

Wheeler was born in Glasgow, Scotland, on September 10, 1890, and named Robert Eric Mortimer, although the last was the name he used. The family soon moved to Edinburgh, where a sister, Amy, was born two years later. His father, Robert Wheeler, was a lecturer in English literature, with a great interest, also, in music and art. During the next few years, he drifted into journalism and the family moved to Yorkshire, settling near the town of Bradford, where he became assistant editor of a local newspaper.

In Mortimer Wheeler's memory, his father was a giant, beloved figure—good-looking, impractical, captivating, and with an "inner spring of happiness." His life was lived in a narrow sphere, but his mind was adventurous: "a scholarly map full of exciting discovery." He had a passion for brave deeds and daring heroes, and little patience for what he saw as weakness.

Father and son were closely bound. On wet afternoons they explored Robert Wheeler's double-stacked bookshelves, as he read aloud and explained whatever came to hand. On good days, they walked through the steep Yorkshire moorlands and woods, in search of adventure and knowledge. Even at three, his father expected the child to keep up with his long stride, and with his conversation. They studied the natural world; watching birds, butterflies, and other creatures. From a chance meeting with a gypsy band, they learned about collecting and cooking wild mushrooms—and then sat "grimly waiting for death" after eating them. His father taught him to hunt, fish, and trap on these excursions; while insisting that everything they caught be eaten.

Along with nature, the region offered other treasures to examine—fascinating, scattered relics of the past: a strangely marked stone, a barrow (burial mound), early crosses in a churchyard, broken pieces of Roman pottery in a stream near an ancient fort, flint knives and scrapers. Wheeler later wrote that these early experiences introduced the "insidious poisons" of archeology into his system.

At home, there was his father, his mother Emily, a "courageous but nervous" woman, lively, adoring Amy, and the baby Betty, born when he was eleven. There were many animals: two mongrel collies, a semi-Persian cat, a wood owl, fantail pigeons, hedgehogs, tortoises, guinea pigs, and grass snakes. His mother taught him at home until he started school late, at age nine, perhaps because of the family's limited income.

After school hours he devoted his time to running a magazine and—with three or four friends—going to art classes. Art became a passion and he spent every spare moment expressing himself with oils, pastels, or watercolors. Every thought took on a shape and color (as an example, Friday was yellow) and with his strong pictorial reflex, he often felt himself happily "encloistered in a picture-gallery."

When Wheeler was fourteen, his father took over his newspaper's London office. Wheeler's first two years in London were a time of exploration. He was too young to enter the university so he was given a map of the city, a small daily allowance for food, and told to educate himself. He spent the days wandering and observing, painting, visiting galleries and the Victoria and Albert Museum, to look at watercolors and at the works of Michelangelo, Leonardo da Vinci, and J. M. W. Turner. He continued walking with his father, and also went to concerts, to the news office, and down any other inviting path. Mornings and evenings he studied for college entrance exams.

In 1907, Wheeler began classical studies at University College of the University of London. He studied Greek and Latin, ancient history, and the history of art, along with science, math, and philosophy. But he still aimed to be a painter and also enrolled at the Slade School of Fine Art. However, he left after a year because he realized, with lasting pain, that he would be only a "conventionally accomplished picture maker."

IN THE WORLD

In 1910, not yet twenty, Wheeler graduated with a bachelor's degree—with "four pennies" in his pocket, no money, no idea what he wanted, and no plan for his life. He took a job the school provost offered, as his private secretary. After a short time, he became publications secretary at a slightly higher salary, and started work for a master's degree.

During the next four years Wheeler set a path for his life. He committed himself to archeology and began a career. He later wrote that "by a process of sliding this way and that, I landed up in archeology." But with a solid background in classical studies, with a curiosity about ancient times nurtured in his childhood, and a liking for open-air activity, it was not just a random choice. In 1913 he was awarded a new two-year archeological studentship (the first of its kind, anywhere) by the university. He proposed a study of pottery found in the ruins of Roman settlements in the region of the Rhine River.

At the time, there was growing interest in studying the remains of Roman Britain. The Romans invaded Britain in the first century B.C. and remained, building forts, outposts, and civilian settlements, until the early fifth century. Archeologists had learned that pottery was an invaluable tool for dating purposes. Shards, or pieces of everyday pots and dishes, were often scattered through ancient sites and provided information for the dating of the area. As Wheeler wrote: "Modern excavation is rightly learning more and more to piece together the history of Roman Britain from its potsherds." Working in a new area of study seemed to Wheeler to offer good opportunities.

With his meager studentship, Wheeler set off for Germany. Both his knowledge of Roman history and his training in drawing were strong assets, and his notes included fine sketches of the Roman pots and other objects in the German museum collections.

When Wheeler returned to England, he found there were few jobs in archeology. He managed to be hired as a junior investigator with the British Royal Commission on Historical Monuments, although he had to enroll in night classes in architecture, to study "the elements of building construction and architectural drawing." He later recommended this training to prospective archeologists.

He muddled through his first assignment—to study and make drawings of a parish church—unfamiliar with the stonework and carvings of medieval church architecture. But for his next project, he was well prepared by his interests and academic training: he was to make a survey of all the Roman remains in the county of Essex.

In the early summer of 1914 he married Tessa Verney whom he had met while both were at University College. She had studied history and became his partner in excavations and other projects, and a respected archeologist in her own right.

Then, in the beginning of August, World War I broke out, with the suddenness of a flash flood, and lives and careers were swept away throughout Europe. Wheeler volunteered early, and joined the University of London Officer Training Corps. He spent three years as an instructor and battery commander in England and Scotland. During this time, a son, Michael, was born. In 1917 he went overseas with the rank of major, thrust into the terrible ongoing slaughter. At the end of the war he returned to London, physically unscarred but deeply wounded by the loss of many comrades. He later wrote of his feeling that a whole generation of fellow historians and archeologists had been lost, and that he—a fortunate survivor—had a debt to help create and train the next generation.

Wheeler found it hard to fit back into his modest junior-investigator position, but picked up his work, examining the Roman imperial past, above and below ground. An amateur explorer took him to see some "dungeons" beneath a nearby Norman castle. With a flash of insight (grounded in his classical and architectural education and his trained visual memory), he realized the dungeon tunnels were actually vaulting supporting a Roman temple. He soon established it was a huge temple built by the conquering emperor Claudius, after a major invasion of A.D. 43.

Wheeler's report of this discovery was published the next year, 1921, quickly laying the foundation for his reputation as a Roman archeologist. He also completed his thesis and earned his doctorate degree. Eager to move ahead, he won a joint position as Keeper of Archaeology in the National Museum of Wales, and Lecturer in Archaeology at the University College of South Wales and Monmouthshire, in Cardiff. He was sorry to leave London—which he saw as the place the profession of archaeology could develop—but Wales offered a challenge and an opportunity.

DIGGING IN WALES

Wheeler had come to believe that any advance in knowledge of the human past depended on "fresh and methodical" discovery—and that meant new digging, excavation. But he also believed that the excavation techniques being used were inadequate and that excavation plans were random and lacked purpose. The excavators could have been "digging up potatoes." He wanted to see excavators following a plan, and working toward "controlled discovery." Only this way could archeology uncover the human past and become a "new instrument for the reconstruction and writing of history."

In thinking about how to improve archeological methods and standards, and set a direction that included historical objectives, he turned to the work of an earlier excavator, Lieutenant-General Augustus Henry Pitt-Rivers, from the last decades of the nineteenth century. Pitt-Rivers had outlined principles that Wheeler now adopted, and followed through his career:

1. A dig director was responsible for training a team of assistants, and for seeing that no excavating was done without expert supervision.

2. The purpose of excavation required careful observation and recording of all the stratification levels and of all materials uncovered, with their exact location in the stratification levels noted.

3. Every observation and detail must be recorded. Often excavators recorded only what seemed to them to be important, omitting other material. But what seemed unimportant at one time could be essential evidence later, as historical knowledge grew.

4. Complete and accurate reports of every excavation must be promptly published.

The fact that these precepts seem so obvious today, so unsurprising, shows how thoroughly they have become part of our expectations. But this was not true in Wheeler's time. Along with establishing standards, these precepts took archeology along a new direction. Archeology was now to be seen as a source of history, and as an academic subject.

The Wheelers spent the next six years in Cardiff. As keeper for the National Museum, and later its director, Wheeler built public support, and actually created the museum—which was little more than an uncompleted building when he arrived. He wrote his first book for the general reader: *Prehistoric and Roman Wales,* "scribbled hastily in trains and country inns." It was a survey of ancient Wales from the time of the cave dwellers through the Roman era. As the first lecturer in archeology, he worked toward establishing the subject in the curriculum of the Welsh university. It was his novel idea that the museum should also play a part in the educational system of the country. In his third role, he continued and advanced his excavating, hoping to add to recorded history.

When the Romans moved into Wales, they built a network of roads linked by forts to control the area. In 1921 Wheeler led his first major excavation, of one of these forts at Segontium. He set to work eagerly, with Tessa as his collaborator. He began to perfect the "Wheeler method" of recording stratification. Each carefully cut section was recorded in detail. Each strata or layers was outlined, filled in with symbols indicating the type of soil, or stones, or other material—all numbered, named, and interpreted. Any found objects were drawn into the diagram. He wrote: "I like to see my sections plastered from head to foot with orderly arrays of labels." Remembering the importance of publishing his findings, he produced prompt excavation reports illustrated with his own clear sectional drawings. And at this first dig, he began the practice of including students in the work; supervising, instructing, and inspiring them with his own enthusiasm and energy.

In 1926 he excavated a Roman fortress at Caerleon. Outside this fortress was a large oval "hollow" which local people called "King Arthur's Round Table," associating the area with the legendary hero of the Middle Ages. It was actually an amphitheater, used by the Romans as a training ground and a place for entertainments; but Wheeler, who was becoming a skilled promoter, saw an opportunity to raise funds for the dig. He sent the press word of his plans, and the next day a representative of the *Daily Mail,* a popular paper, arrived. The paper would finance the excavation of "King Arthur's Round Table" in return for exclusive daily reports. Howard Carter's discovery of Tutankhamen's tomb in Egypt (1922) had aroused great public interest, and newspapers hoped to attract readers with bulletins about other amazing discoveries. Wheeler felt that the archeologist had a responsibility to share knowledge with the public; to educate and interest people in the human past. And he welcomed the funding that would allow him to do his work. Some of the publicity centered on him—a forceful man with a powerful personality, and he enjoyed it.

As his museum and excavation projects were going well, Wheeler began to concentrate on a new plan—to create a university institute of archeology, to provide systematic training for the field. In 1926, Wheeler was offered a position as keeper at the London Museum and jumped at the chance to move back to London—exactly where he felt the institute should be located, with the blueprint for it in his pocket.

TO LONDON, WITH A PLAN

Wheeler arrived in London with a list of goals: to reform and revitalize the poorly staffed, disorganized museum—he called it a junk shop; to conduct excavations to increase knowledge, improve techniques, and bring glory to British archeology; to get recognition of archeology as an academic subject and start training students; and to found an Institute of Archaeology. He believed archeology should be a postgraduate field, so that students would have a broad knowledge of history. With enormous energy and ability, Wheeler managed to do all of this—although it would take ten years to establish the institute. Throughout, he relied on Tessa, whose administrative abilities and soothing nature often carried him through difficult times until she died, suddenly, in 1936. Wheeler remarried twice, but not happily.

In April 1937 the Institute of Archaeology was launched, to provide "materials for study, instruction in the treatment of antiquities, and training in archeological methods in research and in the recording of research." Wheeler saw an even larger purpose: archeology was the study of human achievement, but its "ultimate function," was the recreation of human life.

The archaeological excavator is not digging up things, he is digging up people; however much he may analyse and tabulate and desiccate his discoveries in the laboratory, the ultimate appeal across the ages, whether the time-interval be 500 or 5,000,000 years, is from mind to intelligent mind. . . . Too often we dig up mere things, unrepentantly forgetful that our proper aim is to dig up people.

The Institute taught techniques of excavation and fieldwork; prehistory, Asian studies, geochronology (archeological environment), Prehistoric, Biblical, Roman and Near Eastern Archeology; and archeological photography, conservation, and repair of antiquities, soil analysis, and much more. Students participated in fieldwork under experienced archeologists including Mortimer Wheeler, "lord of the trench and earthworks," who was happiest when, dressed in digging clothes and spade in hand, he could explore human history.

During these active years, Wheeler led a systematic series of excavations. As he explored Roman Britain, he did not stop at excavating each site, but interpreted it and constructed a picture of its life. His report on the excavation of Lydney Park in Gloucestershire (1928-29) re-created the civilian life of the pre-Roman inhabitants—Celts—and their survival under Roman rule about the first century B.C. and later. It explained the site and its importance; and presented plans, sectional descriptions, drawings of mosaics and other finds, and even sketches of the inhabitants and wildlife.

Wheeler next excavated Verulamium, a Roman civilian town near London, now known as St. Albans. He coordinated information from written history (references by classical writers, including Julius Caesar) with "testimony from the spade," gained in four seasons of fieldwork, to reconstruct its life through four and a half centuries.

Tessa Wheeler, in the center of the photograph, supervises students excavating pit dwellings at Maiden Castle.

In 1934 Wheeler began a major excavation of Maiden Castle, an Iron-Age hill fort near Dorchester. He explored the vast site using his new grid system of horizontal trenches. His excavation report, *Maiden Castle, Dorset,* is a classic in archeology. Wheeler's exciting blow-by-blow description of the final assault by the Roman Legions after the invasion of A.D. 43 incorporates Roman sources and shows readers the evidence—the arrowheads and battle axes, tumbled stone walls and burned huts, graves with tribute food and scarred skeletons, coins, pottery fragments, and all the other unearthed data—from which he constructed his dramatic account.

When World War II began Wheeler volunteered and served two years in North Africa and Italy. While in Algiers, in August 1943, he

This archeologist is cleaning a skeleton excavated at Maiden Castle, near Dorchester. Archeologists found that a battle had taken place there in A.D. 43.

received the bombshell message—asking him to be Director-General of Archeology in India. In early 1944 he sailed in a military convoy and stepped ashore in Bombay, "with a mind full of ill-digested Indian history but with a pretty clear plan of campaign," to take on this challenging job: to oversee the huge land mass of the Indian subcontinent, to preserve its ancient sites and buildings, to carry out excavation, to manage its museums, to develop a history of the vast region, to publish reports and monographs, and to educate the public about the material and cultural heritage of India.

DIGGING IN ASIA

The British had gained control of the Indian subcontinent in the seventeenth century and gradually incorporated it into the British Empire. In time, a movement for self-determination grew and England agreed to grant independence as of August 1947. The country would be partitioned along religious and ethnic lines; with the largest part becoming India (a primarily Hindu nation), and two separate areas in the northwest and northeast forming Pakistan (primarily Muslim). In 1971 the northeast portion broke off from Pakistan to become Bangladesh.

When Wheeler arrived, with an appointment to serve for four years, India was preparing for independence and partition. He had headquarters, often shared with invading monkeys, in a railway board building in Simla, with a view of the mountains. His assistants warned him to slow down and not fight the midday heat. But Wheeler was too aware of his limited time and announced he would "ignore" the climate. He described his arrival in words from the Revelation of St. John: " The Devil is come down amongst you having great wrath, because he knoweth that he hath but a short time." He set to work with a roar, enjoying his authority, knowing he had the skills, and "amazed by the glory that is India."

His goals remained the same: to excavate and research, and train students; plus the challenge of formulating a coherent history of Indian civilization and searching for the legacy of the Indus civilization on later cultures. The world had long known about the ancient civilizations of Greece, Rome, Egypt, and Mesopotamia. But even today, people in the West are often not as aware of the ancient cultures of Asia. The Indus Valley civilization was the earliest urban culture on the Indian subcontinent; deposits go back as far as 3300 B.C. and the area seems to have been continuously inhabited ever since. It reached its height in the 3rd millennium B.C., and corresponds to the Bronze Age cultures of ancient Egypt, Mesopotamia, and Crete. The two capital cities—Harappa, in the Punjab, and Mohenjo-daro, on the Indus River—were located in the 1920s and 1930s. Early excavations revealed that an advanced civilization had existed, spreading over an enormous area through the Indus Valley (in what is now Pakistan), westward to today's Iranian border, and as far east as New Delhi, and to the Oxus River in northern Afghanistan—one of the largest areas covered by a single Bronze Age culture.

The early archeologists believed Harappa and Mohenjo-daro were unfortified cities, with no palaces or temples. But Wheeler, following instinct, quickly figured out that the high mounds of yellow mud were eroded mud-brick walls, the fortifications of the cities. Using his square method of excavation, and working through the blazing afternoons, his workers uncovered well-planned cities, with public buildings, drainage systems, granaries, peasant homes, and workshops. His work reversed some earlier interpretations and, although some of his conclusions are now questioned, he believed it provided historical foundation for the collection of Hindu Sanskrit writings, the *Rigved*, which described Aryan invaders sweeping into India about 1500 B.C., led by a leader called the "fort-destroyer," who "destroyed ninety forts and a hundred ancient castles."

Wheeler also set up a training school—the first true training school in world archeology—which was later widely copied. His students came from throughout the subcontinent, to study excavation and recording, surveying, photography, and administration. Wheeler enjoyed their diversity: Muslims, Bengalis, Madrasis, southerners from Cochin and Travancore; while fearing that religious and political barriers would end

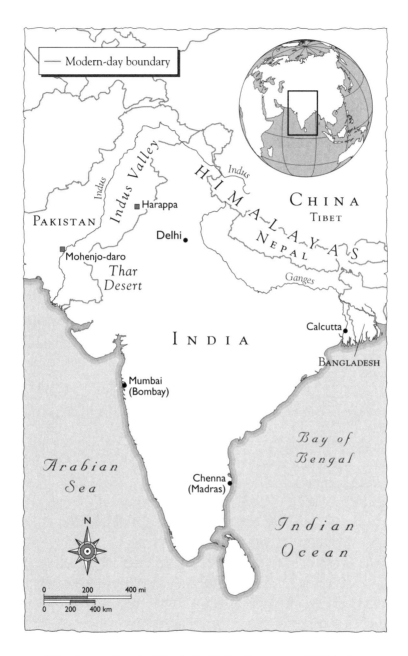

Mortimer Wheeler explored in The Indus Valley. As early as 2500 B.C., civilization flourished in what is now Pakistan and Western India.

this easy cooperation after partition. And, although strict and demanding, he enjoyed their devotion and curiosity. One extraordinary night when snow fell, a southern student was seen stuffing some into his pockets—to send home to his parents who had never seen the substance.

Wheeler worked to set up the Indian National Museum, which is now a treasure of New Delhi. He led successful excavations in both north and south India, uncovered ancient periods of occupation, and established a chronology for the whole peninsula. Wheeler also found the first pre-Indus Valley civilization deposits and demonstrated trading patterns and contacts with Rome and other areas.

Through bouts of malaria, enduring heat and rainy seasons, and bureaucratic inefficiency, Wheeler worked himself, his staff, and students hard. In 1945, World War II ended, which had little impact on Wheeler's activities. But in 1947, as India moved toward its Independence Day, disorder and violence increased. After August 15, 1947 when British flags were taken down, he planned to leave. He made rounds of inspection and farewell, fearing that all his work would be swept away. But in Karachi, capital of the new state of Pakistan, he was encouraged when the Minister of Education asked him to return to Pakistan as Archeological Adviser to the government for a number of months during the next three years. He left with regret, but knew he had achieved much and hoped the generation of native archeologists he had trained would continue the work.

A VARIETY OF NEW CAREERS

In 1948 Wheeler returned to London, resumed teaching at the Institute of Archaeology and became Honorary Secretary to the British Academy. He participated in some digs in England and was kept busy lecturing and being honored. He gave a series of lectures in the United States for the Archeological Institute of America. He also took an active and enthusiastic part in establishing British Schools Overseas, specifically an Institute of History and Archeology in East

Africa and the British Institute of Persian Studies in Teheran. He was knighted by Queen Elizabeth in 1952.

The last phase of Wheeler's career may have been the busiest. In 1952 a television producer adapted an American program, "What in the World?" for British television. It was a quiz show in which museums challenged the panel of experts (including Wheeler) to identify mysterious objects from their collections. The program, renamed "Animal, Vegetable, Mineral?" became wildly popular. Wheeler, with his assurance and flair, became the star—instinctively knowing that the audience didn't want to see him pick up something and say "this is a Samoan cake mold." They wanted to watch an expert work through to a decision. Wheeler had a great fund of knowledge and his excellent visual memory to help him. In 1954, the series' second year, Wheeler was chosen "Television Personality of the Year." He also continued lecturing and writing; eager to educate the public in human history. His *Archaeology from the Earth* would become the authoritative field guide to archeology. *Still Digging*, his autobiography, was published in 1955.

Wheeler and Dr. Nash Williams, scientist at the National Museum of Wales, examine pottery excavated in Wales.

Wheeler never gave up the idea of finding out more about the past. Here, he investigates discoveries at an archeological dig in London.

The "Animal, Vegetable, Mineral?" series led to other popular projects: radio talks for "The Archeologist," a "Buried Treasure" television series, programs on African prehistory, and a three-part "The Grandeur that was Rome." They reached an enormous audience, popularizing archeology and leading to another activity. In 1954 Wheeler was invited to join a Hellenic cruise as lecturer. The Swans of London agency was offering Greek and Roman cruises led by classical scholars. Wheeler became a popular speaker and guide—eloquent, dashing, knowledgeable, and always able to add a personal anecdote. He saw all these activities as ways to involve the public in the exploration of the past. And he enjoyed the celebrity that accompanied them. He gradually became an unofficial public-relations officer for the field of archeology until his death in 1976.

Kathleen Kenyon, an archeologist who trained under Wheeler, wrote of his importance both as an excavator and innovator in excavation techniques, but added that his greatest strength was his ability to go to the heart of interpreting a site. He is remembered as one of the greatest of twentieth-century archeologists, and his advice to his students remains as useful today as in his time: "Have a plan. And . . . see that the plan is worthwhile, is likely to add significantly to our knowledge of the human mind and human achievement."

Sir Mortimer Wheeler is regarded as one of the greatest archeologists of the twentieth century.

Chapter 6

"BOUNTIFUL GODS SHOWERED GIFTS UPON THE LAND"

GERTRUDE BELL AND KATHLEEN KENYON EXPLORE THE MIDDLE EAST

Gertrude Bell was independent, and not easily frightened. She was at ease traveling in the desert almost on her own—the only woman in a party of soldiers and muleteers. She had written one book with the desert as its setting. Now, in 1909, she had another project in mind, as she set out on a daring excursion, from Syria to Mesopotamia—to explore the ancient land between the two rivers, the Tigris and the Euphrates.

The group traveled for some time, not certain what was ahead but curious to see what the desert might reveal. Suddenly, a huge castle arose before their eyes, its mighty walls seemingly created from the sand. From her research, Bell realized that this was the late eighth-century walled palace of Ukhaidir—a site she had long hoped to find.

Intrigued by the huge castle and its fortified enclosure, she approached slowly. To her delight, she and her crew were greeted warmly by the sheikhs who stayed there. Recognizing her respect for

Ukhaidir, which Bell felt was "the work of nature, not of man," they allowed her to spend days surveying and photographing the site. She could not wait to announce her discovery of this vanished civilization to the wider world.

Bell's Middle East explorations—and those of Kathleen Kenyon, a later archeologist—were highly considered, but this was not always the case for female explorers. For although women have played an important role in twentieth-century archeology, they have not been given the credit they deserve for some very significant finds. Too often they were assigned roles secondary to the directors of the digs; while they put forth ample effort as field workers, even supervisors, only rarely did they create their own archeological history.

Gertrude Bell and Kathleen Kenyon are exceptions to this rule. Born more than a century apart, each gained recognition for her achievements in the region of the world we know today as the Middle East—where men had previously been involved in most major excavations. Both women were awarded the Order of the British Empire by their Queens (Mary and Elizabeth, respectively), among other honors, and had the satisfaction of knowing that they had made important contributions to Middle Eastern prehistory.

A BACKGROUND OF PRIVILEGE AND POWER

Gertrude Margaret Lowthian Bell was born in 1868 in Durham County, England, the daughter of a wealthy Yorkshire businessman. She was descended, on her paternal side, from men who combined abilities in science and business with concern for social reform. These were men who could run a thriving business and spend stimulating evenings with the great philosophers of the day while still speaking out on public health and education. Her grandfather, and to a greater extent, her father, were Gertrude's role models—from them she inherited keen intelligence, drive, and a sense of curiosity about the world.

The child's early years were happy, living in luxury with loving parents. It was a tribute to her father's warmth and attention that the child did not have a sense of abandonment when her mother died soon after the birth of her brother. All of her life, Gertrude sought her father's admiration and thought of him as the epitome of wisdom and understanding.

In the custom of the time, the young woman was first educated at home, but her exceptional mind compelled her father and step-mother to send her to a girl's school in London. Lonely and unhappy in the single-sex institution, she asked to continue her history studies at Oxford University. When she entered Oxford in 1886, she delighted in being one of the few "girls" among hundreds of men—as she would throughout her life. Just as important, the hard work at Oxford was exciting and stimulating. When she graduated, Bell was awarded one of Oxford's primary honors—a First in Modern History—the first woman to achieve this distinction.

FIGHTING VICTORIAN MORES

Living in England at a time when women were supposed to marry young and then disappear into their husbands' households, the unmarried Bell found travel a special escape and adventure. After graduation she left on a trip to Romania, and then to Persia (modern Iran), where she had her first taste of the Middle East. When she traveled to Europe and the Far East in 1897-98 she found a new outlet for this love of risk—mountain climbing. She found the challenge absorbing and fun, and became one of the outstanding mountain-climbers of her generation.

But back home in England, where women of her class did not enjoy adventure or hold jobs, Bell was bored. Soon she was off again, this time to Rome and then to Athens. It was in Greece that she watched a friend working at a dig, extracting 6,000-year-old vessels from the earth. She was also fascinated by stories of archeologists on the scene, who described the ancient world found from the excavations—pots and shards and rocks. Bell suddenly realized that she had found a field that could be important to her life.

By 1899 she was off to Jerusalem, where she stayed for seven months; it was the beginning of an intense emotional and professional connection with the Arab people. Visiting with old friends, she resumed the study of Arabic begun on her earlier trip to Persia. According to Janet Wallach, author of *Desert Queen—the Life of Gertrude Bell*, "her goal was to enter the Arab world." Comfortable with the Arabic language, she determined to travel the land, and headed into the desert on her horse. Bell was not alone—she was accompanied by a hired cook, two muleteers and a guide, as well as a soldier—but she was the only woman in the group, as she was often to be.

LIVING IN TWO WORLDS

For the next years, Bell divided her time between England and the Middle East. By 1902, she had joined an archeological dig on the island of Malta, then visited Jerusalem, where she was warmly welcomed. It was at this time in her life that she realized that in the Middle East, unlike London, she could be a "person." It was a mutual affection: she

While most women of her era usually stayed at home, Gertrude Bell traveled throughout the world in search of archeological discoveries.

could be well received there throughout the rest of her life, and she would enjoy these very different people. Unlike the English, they stimulated her imagination, with their romantic, exotic, and mysterious ways.

Gertrude Bell was particularly at home with the *Druze* (modern "Druse") people of Syria, a Muslim sect that combined teachings of Islam, Buddhism, Christianity, and Judaism. She spent much time with them in the desert, and they were charmed by her—at one point they dubbed her an "honorary man," their highest honor. Wanting the English to know about the Druze, she wrote a book on the subject, *The Desert and the Sown*. The work was published in 1907 to critical praise and popular success. *The Times* of London, the *Times Literary Supplement*, and *The New York Times* all hailed the book; one critic called it among the dozen best books of Eastern travel.

Bell continued to have many adventures in the desert. Riding for hours across the dusty landscape, she was attired like any proper Englishwoman—frilly blouses and tweed jackets, a fur coat, silver brushes, and cut glass bottles for her lotions—along with maps, cameras, film, binoculars, and guns. (She hid the bullets in her shoes, to evade detection by border guards.) In 1909, planning to do research on another book, she began her journey from Syria to Mesopotamia—again a sole woman traveling with several male servants and muleteers and soldiers—encountering groups of Arabs of whom she had no fear.

It was during this trip she came upon the most important relic of its period—the walled palace the Arabs called Ukhaidir, "a little green place." It was actually neither small nor green. The huge late eighth-century castle in a fortified enclosure had never been identified; Bell set out to be the first to bring the spectacular ruin to public attention.

Photographing, sketching, measuring, and drawing the plan of the castle to scale, she was lost in her work. Bell was convinced that this was a major archeological find, and that it might bring her fame and glory. But, sadly, in Constantinople (Istanbul), the last stop of her journey home, she discovered that a French archeologist, Mr. Massignon, had recently written about Ukhaidir in the magazine *Gazette des Beaux Arts*.

It was a bitter disappointment, but Bell put it behind her and moved on. She published *Amurath to Amurath*, a chronicle of her Mesopotamian archeological journey. The book was well reviewed, but not as favorably as *The Desert and the Sown*. During a 1911 trip to revisit ruins of the Hittite people, a powerful empire that thrived from 2000 to 1200 B.C., she met T. E. Lawrence. Lawrence was a twenty-three-year-old graduate student on one of his first expeditions, already fascinated by Arabian customs and dress. He would achieve almost mythic fame as Lawrence of Arabia.

USING HER DESERT EDUCATION FOR ENGLAND

Bell had become very knowledgeable about the desert—hazards such as lack of water to drink, flooding in odd places, freezing cold nights and blazing hot days, snakes, scorpions, and sand—and the habits of the desert Arabs. She also consulted with her native friends, from sheikhs to mule-drivers, to learn even more.

She had begun to realize that she could be of use to the British government during the imminent war, beyond Red Cross work. The Turks had allied with the Germans, and there was a strong need for Bell's ability to map Northern Arabia. She had hoped to do this earlier, but was seen as threatening to the male government leaders. Then, as World War I loomed, she suddenly had an important job to do, and was accepted for her special skills.

Bell's first project was in Egypt. Working diligently, she was able to catalog the Arab clans, campsites, water wells, topography, and terrain, as well as the lineage of sheikhs, their personalities, feuds, and strengths. She then moved to India, where her job was to gather information from the Arabs and serve as a liaison between British Intelligence in Cairo and Indian Intelligence in New Delhi. Then she worked in Basrah, near Baghdad, in Iraq, and became the only female Political Officer in the British Forces.

By 1917 Bell was able to go back to Baghdad—this time officially as Oriental Secretary, the key British Intelligence post in the region, as well as Curator of Antiquities. Her role was to analyze the power and politics of local leaders, evaluate the links to enemy Turks, and judge their potential loyalty to the British.

HELPING TO CREATE A NATION

Gertrude Bell played a major role in developing the independent country of Iraq. As Oriental Secretary, she was in a powerful position, helping to decide how it would be governed, its laws and institutions. There were questions of whether to install an Arab king to rule or to keep firm British authority over the people. Driven by nationalism which was to strengthen over the next decades, the Arabs wanted to be in charge of their own nation. Many Arabs loved Gertrude, but others accused her of trying to keep their emerging nation under British domination.

After the war, Bell turned again to archeology. In 1921 she joined a group from Chicago's Field Museum at the site of Kish in Southern Iraq, along with a joint team that had arrived from the British Museum and the University of Pennsylvania Museum to excavate in Iraq. As the Honorary Director of Archeology, Bell took great interest in inspecting the sites. She was particularly impressed by work being done at the ancient Sumerian city of Ur, biblical birthplace of Abraham, which had flourished nearly six thousand years earlier. Its mound offered archeological riches that were outstanding. It yielded information about all aspects of Sumerian life, from ziggurats (staggered, staircased towers of 2000 B.C.) to thin, curved canoes, to spectacular treasures in the royal tombs. These included golden statuettes, golden headdresses, golden daggers with lapis lazuli hilts, copper vases, and tablets with cuneiform inscriptions.

Thrilled by all of these discoveries, Gertrude Bell made a decision that would have a major impact on the archeological history of Iraq: she formulated a law of excavation to protect the nation from being robbed of the treasures she was sure would be found in the future, as well as those then being now. She also stood up to natives when she found them scavenging the archeological finds. Paying a fair price for the objects, she brought them back to the new Iraq Museum of Antiquities in Baghdad, which she helped to develop.

As Curator of Antiquities, she had a valuable position—she had the right of first claim to any treasures for the Iraqi government. She took the finds to the museum, where she toiled with scholarly patience, gluing fragments, identifying and cataloging the objects, and overseeing workers who did not have the concern she did about correct labeling. Once, Bell noticed a small fragment of a horse's neck and mane labeled "portion of a man's shoulder," which she quickly corrected.

Before she died, in 1926, Gertrude Bell had the joy of seeing the Iraq Museum moved from the government building where it had been housed into its own structure. On her death, she left fifty thousand pounds to the museum; she hoped to further its work of collecting and displaying the archeology of the nation. She had realized through her years in the Middle East that the achievements of the early Mesopotamians, the ancestors of the modern Iraqis, were outstanding. The more proof she had of these achievements, gained through archeological excavation, the more strongly she felt that Iraq would some day return to its former greatness.

GROWING UP WITH ANTIQUITIES

Like Gertrude Bell, who had a father of singular intellect, Kathleen Kenyon learned early the value of scholarship for a rich and full life. But even more than Gertrude Bell, Kathleen Kenyon lived surrounded by the antiquities that would become the basis for her life's work. Her father, Sir Frederick Kenyon, was an eminent biblical scholar who was named director of the British Museum, the world's leading treasury of archeology.

Born in London in 1906, Kathleen was an early achiever—becoming a top student (known as "head girl") at St Paul's Girls' School. At Somerville College, Oxford, she was the first female president of the Oxford Archaeological Society, and realized she had found her life's work. After a well-rounded college career which

Kathleen Kenyon led expeditions to excavate some sites in England where ancient Romans had built cities.

included hockey and history along with her archeology activities, Kathleen Kenyon graduated in 1929.

In the late 1920s, archeology was becoming a science. Soon after she left Oxford, Kenyon went off on her first excavation as a member of Dr. Gertrude Caton-Thompson's expedition to Southern Rhodesia (now Zimbabwe). The young woman had the opportunity to learn the techniques of excavation under the outstanding archeologist Caton-Thompson, and to supervise her own first expedition and contribute to its report.

Soon after returning to London, Kenyon began a long association with the renowned archeologist Mortimer Wheeler. She joined his staff in an excavation of the Roman town at Verulamium, near

London, in England. Beginning as a trainee, she soon showed the acuteness of observation and independence of judgment that would distinguish her later work and bring her international fame.

A NEW WAY TO EXCAVATE

The work at Verulamiun culminated in the uncovering of a Roman theater that is now a public monument—the only visible structure of its kind in England. As important, Kathleen Kenyon learned Wheeler's new method of stratigraphic excavation: excavating by trenches, which requires careful observation, interpretation, and recording throughout the digging project. This method of recording and drawing to scale usually allows for plotting in three dimensions the positions and relationships of finds, and assigning relative dates to them.

Kenyon was assigned to supervise some of the more difficult and tedious parts of the expedition, but did not complain. She was coming into her own as an expedition leader, learning to command the work force with an attitude of authority and force of character. And she was developing administrative skills that would be useful throughout her professional career.

During 1931-34, Kenyon made her first excursion to the Middle East, joining the excavation of a site in Sumer, in southern Mesopotamia, under the direction of a well-known archeologist, John Crowfoot. The excavation was of particular interest because the Sumerians were one of the world's oldest civilizations, credited with the invention of cuneiform writing, the plow, and wheeled vehicles. In this project, the young woman introduced some of the more advanced techniques that were being developed in British archeology, but were rarely seen in other countries.

This expedition also gave Kathleen Kenyon her first knowledge of the land then known as Palestine, and she developed a lifelong affection for both place and people. Like Gertrude Bell, she became fascinated by the natives of the desert. Their struggles would become her concerns as she worked to uncover the early history of biblical lands.

This photo shows Kenyon and an assistant examining pieces of Roman pottery discovered in an ancient site that is now called St. Albans. At this site, they discovered the ruins of a theater with an outer wall and an entrance to the stage.

Back in England in 1935, she contributed to the founding of the University of London's Institute of Archaeology, becoming its secretary, then acting director. During World War II, she remained in England, exploring prehistoric hill-forts in Herefordshire. After the war, she began to lecture in Palestinian archeology at the Institute of Archaeology, which she had almost single-handedly kept running throughout the war. She also did field work in a variety of locations, in England and Italy.

By 1951 she was headed back to the Middle East, where she was appointed honorary director of the British School of Archaeology in Jerusalem. With the permission and generous support of the Department of Antiquities of the Hashemite Kingdom of Jordan, as well as the Minister of Education of the Jordan and Palestine Archaeology Museum, Kathleen Kenyon moved into the expedition that made her famous—digging into the thirty-eight-hundred-year-old "mound" of Jericho, a region that is now the Hashemite Kingdom of Jordan.

Archeologists uncovered a Roman theater at Verulamium, near London, England

EARLY CIVILIZATIONS UNEARTHED

The results of Kenyon's work—from 1952 to 1958—reshaped our understanding of the earlier phases of civilization. In fact, the discoveries revolutionized prehistoric chronology of that part of the world. Her excavation into the lower levels of the Jericho city mound, plus use of new dating techniques, radically changed the popular view about the beginnings of farming.

Some years before, archeologist John Garstang had dug trenches deep into the *tell* (mound) of Jericho, exposing Bronze Age levels and traces of even earlier Stone Age farming occupation. In her no-nonsense way, Kenyon ran a large-scale excavation. She re-opened

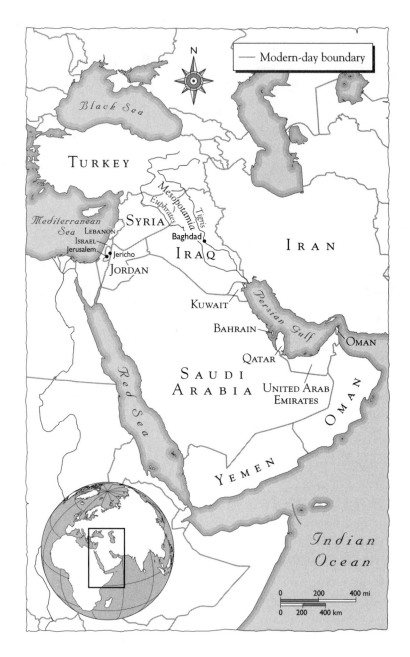

Both Bell and Kenyon made remarkable discoveries in the Middle East. This map shows some of the locations of their discoveries.

Kenyon and her assistants excavated a site at Jericho. The ancient walls of the city are more than 3,000 years old.

the trenches that Garstang had carelessly excavated and poorly reported, then dug down to the base of the biblical city, known not only as the oldest town of the world, but the lowest—nine hundred feet below sea level, in the great rift of the Jordan Valley.

As Kenyon and her crew worked, they were surprised to find two farming communities, complete with stone walls, a watch tower, and a small shrine near a spring. They sent samples of the community's artifacts to a University of Chicago laboratory for the new technique of radiocarbon dating, which would establish a dating sequence of the time period for the site. With the results, the workers realized they had discovered early agricultural life from the eighth and seventh millennia B.C.—earlier than estimates for early agriculture, which were closer to 4000 B.C.

A FLOURISHING TOWN

The discoveries in the Jericho excavation, 1952-56, were remarkable. At a time when other peoples were nomadic hunters, Jericho was a real town surrounded by an imposing stone wall. It was clear that an organized and flourishing community lived there. Among many startling features was the technique for burial of the ancient people; the remains were very well preserved. But Kenyon believed that the greatest discovery was the town's spring, created by natural underground reservoirs fed by rain in the Judean hills, which gushes forth to irrigate the fields of Jericho. This is doubtless the reason settlers were attracted to the site thousands of years ago. Even today, the spring provides waters for life in Jordan.

Kathleen Kenyon was interested in the excavation of Jericho because of its historic importance. In the introduction to her book *Digging Up Jericho*, she noted the long-held view that "the very origins of civilisation are to be sought in the Fertile Crescent. These origins lie in the first steps towards settled life, which is characteristic of the Neolithic Period . . . the revolutionary step forward was the discovery that wild grains could be cultivated . . . wild animals herded . . . and the growth of fixed settlements become possible." (The Fertile Crescent is the crescent-shaped area of fertile land in the ancient Middle East—from Mesopotamia to Assyria, westward to the Mediterranean, and south through Palestine to the Nile Valley.)

In going about the work, Kenyon described the main difference between the techniques she was using and those used earlier: the more detailed supervision of actual removal of material. The soil was to be carefully removed, in layers, and recorded, as well as interpreted as to the significance of the layers. So professional field supervisors were vital, as were surveyors, photographers, draftsmen, and technicians, among others.

Because the project was difficult and tiring, Kenyon scheduled the expedition for a three-month "season," January through April, for each of its four years. This was as much to allow time to recoup energy as to collect the funds needed for staff and supplies. Despite Kathleen Kenyon's growing reputation, it was still difficult to finance archeological projects.

Yet despite the taxing aspects of both the work and the fund-raising, the finds were obviously worth the labor. At one point, Kenyon's crew members finally unearthed the human skulls they had seen traces of several years before, on the side of a trench. The family grouping of seven heads, each with a strongly marked individual character, were covered for preservation in plaster, with shells placed in the eye sockets.

The crew leader believed that these were the heads of honored ancestors of the community—preserved as portraits to show the faces to people in later times. Further digging disclosed many skeletons in oval-shaped houses; a large number of the skeletons had skulls removed, as if, Kenyon believed, there was an idea of a spiritual life distinct from a bodily one.

The Jericho expedition would be a hard act to follow, and indeed Kenyon's next project, a dig in Jerusalem, proved less rewarding. There were several reasons, including the 1967 Six-Day War, a short but fierce conflict between Arabs and Israelis, fought less than twenty years after the birth of the State of Israel. The war interrupted the work, but the fact that the site was not as interesting archeologically was another factor in the less successful Jerusalem excavation.

During the 1960s, Kathleen had a falling out with her mentor Mortimer Wheeler. He felt she demonstrated a pro-Arab bias, because of her part in helping to formulate a UNESCO resolution against Israeli excavations in Jerusalem. There is little doubt that most of the staff in the British Institute of Archaeology, including

Kenyon, had pro-Arab sympathies. Kenyon admitted her political involvement with the Arabs, but also noted that she got on well with the Israeli archeologists and had their respect.

MOVING INTO AN ACADEMIC LIFE

When the Jerusalem expedition ended, Kenyon decided by 1973 that she would retire from active archeology, and became principal of St. Hugh's College, Oxford. She also wanted to concentrate on her books, *Digging Up Jericho* and *Digging Up Jerusalem*, which have become almost textbooks in archeology, pointing up the best techniques in all aspects of excavation. While she completed many works before her death in 1978, she left some unfinished, including the last volumes on the Jericho excavation.

That Kenyon was an outstanding archeologist—an expedition leader loved and respected by those who worked with her—is seen from the book *Archaeology in the Levant—Essays for Kathleen Kenyon*, edited from the offerings of her colleagues over the years and printed in 1976 as a gift for her seventieth birthday.

Among many essays was a personal appreciation by Dr. and Mrs. Tushingham, who had served as archeological assistants on the Jericho excavation. Kathleen Kenyon was praised as well-organized, her purposes well-defined, a director who "obviously knew what she was doing and what she required of people by her own zeal, modesty and naturalness, she could make the process of learning a new discipline a pleasant and rewarding experience."

Chapter 7
"THE BIGGEST TOMB IN THE VALLEY"

KENT R. WEEKS AND THE DISCOVERY OF THE BURIAL SITE OF THE SONS OF RAMESSES II

*I*n 1989 Egyptian authorities decided the roadway at the entrance to the Valley of the Kings, a major tourist attraction for hundreds of years, needed to be widened. The plan was to enable tour buses to turn around, instead of having to maneuver backwards down the road, through throngs of tourists and other buses. This plan set off an alarm for Kent R. Weeks, an American archeologist working on a mapping project in the Valley. What if there was something important lying in the path of the earth-levelers?

Quickly, before the machinery was brought in, he began a last-minute excavation of the area. Six years later, Weeks was one hundred feet (30m) inside a mountain, crawling through a narrow tunnel and into what he expected to be a small underground chamber. As his flashlight played over the walls he saw he was in a long corridor that stretched on into the darkness. He could make out doorways lining each wall. "I realized the corridor was tremendous," he recalled later. "There was one door on the left, another on the right, then two more then four . . . sixteen, eighteen. . . . I had never seen a corridor like this in *any* Egyptian tomb. 'This is incredible,' I muttered." With a graduate student and an Egyptian workman, he struggled past fallen blocks and debris, in stifling heat. Their glasses kept fogging up with the humidity, and dust made it hard to breathe. And then, at the end of the corridor, they saw a shadowy, five-foot-high (1.5m) figure: Osiris, god of the afterlife; the god with whom ancient Egyptians were united at death.

As they continued exploring they realized there were more than sixty-five chambers in the tomb. When they finally crawled out, exhausted but exhilarated, they were greeted by their excited workmen, shouting "This is the biggest tomb in the valley! The biggest tomb in the valley!" Weeks's spectacular find was soon revealed to be not only the largest, but also the most complex tomb ever discovered in Egypt, and the burial place of as many as fifty of the sons of Ramesses II, the most important of all the rulers of ancient Egypt.

Kent Weeks and his wife, Susan, examine a hallway inside the KV5 tomb. The hallway is more than one hundred feet (30m) long and is lined with doors leading to chambers.

Tomb-robbers and treasure-seekers had been scavenging through ancient Egypt for centuries. In his day, Giovanni Belzoni believed there were still undiscovered wonders, and in 1817 located six royal tombs, including the splendidly decorated tomb of Seti I. He then declared there were no more tombs to be found. Despite this general belief that the Valley of Kings had given up all its secrets, Howard Carter astonished the world a century later, with the discovery of the tomb of Tutankhamen.

When Kent R. Weeks arrived, in the 1990s, the Valley of Kings had been well picked over. Yet, disregarding advice that there was nothing new to be uncovered, Weeks made one of the most important discoveries of twentieth-century archeology. His discovery of the burial site of the sons of Ramesses II demonstrates that even in a thoroughly explored area, an archeologist with vision and persistence can make amazing discoveries; using traditional tools of intelligence, observation, and careful pick-and-shovel digging, augmented by some newer high-tech approaches.

EGYPTOLOGY—THE GOAL

In the 1940s and 1950s, most eight-year-olds were dreaming about going along on a space mission to Mars, or becoming sports heroes or famous inventors. But Kent R. Weeks, growing up in Everett, Washington (population about twenty-five thousand), knew he wanted to be an Egyptologist. He was gripped by the mystery of the ancient civilization, and longed for the adventure of "cutting open mummies," digging through the sand, and learning the secrets of the pyramids and the treasure-filled tombs. His parents—his father was a policeman and his mother a medical records supervisor—did not discourage his ambition, and fortunately some of his teachers shared his interest and lent him their own books about ancient Egypt. After he exhausted these resources and the local library, he discovered the interlibrary loan system and was soon "ordering Egyptology books from libraries all over western America."

As a high school student in 1956, Weeks met his first Egyptologist in the flesh. Dr. Ahmed Fakhry, a professor at Cairo University, was in the United States accompanying a touring exhibit of some of the magnificent artifacts from the tomb of Tutankhamen. Weeks went to Seattle to see the exhibit and became "almost dizzy with excitement" when Dr. Fakhry responded to his enthusiasm and spent some hours with him, describing his own projects in Egypt and helping Weeks work out a plan for his college studies. Another friendly adviser, a professor at the University of Chicago, provided more encouragement and good advice by mail: "do not specialize too soon; get a good liberal arts education; study foreign languages."

At college, at the University of Washington in Seattle, Weeks chose courses to prepare for the Egyptology career he hoped to have. In *The Lost Tomb*, his account of his work in Egypt, he outlined his college program: "I majored in anthropology and prehistoric archaeology and minored in ancient history and the history of medicine. . . . I also took courses in human anatomy and pathology, English literature, Chinese society, plus Greek and French and German. These turned out to be wise choices."

When Weeks was in his last year at college, the High Dam was about to be constructed at Aswan, on the Nile River. The dam would provide Egypt with needed hydroelectric power and water for irrigation, but the rising river waters would flood thousands of archeological sites and destroy many monuments, including the extraordinary temples of Abu Simbel, built by Ramesses II in Nubia, south of Egypt. Weeks volunteered to join a salvage effort planned by Yale University, to save some of the monuments by moving them to higher ground. He received plane tickets by return mail and in November of 1963 arrived in Egypt for the first time. Over the next few years he returned to Nubia a number of times to work on various projects, including a study of the teeth of Egyptian mummies.

During one of these projects, he re-met a young woman he had known at the University of Washington, Susan Howe, who was now an artist and illustrator working on archeological expeditions. They returned to the United States and married in 1966 and have since worked together on many projects.

Weeks went back to the University of Washington for an M.A. and then to Yale where he completed his Ph.D. in Egyptology in 1970, with a dissertation on ancient Egyptian anatomical terminology. The next move was to New York, where Weeks became assistant curator of Egyptian art at the Metropolitan Museum of Art, and taught in the history department at Queens College of the City University of New York. Susan Weeks took a job as an artist in the Paleontology Department at the American Museum of Natural History.

EXPLORING THEBES

Although these were exciting jobs, both missed Egypt. Two years later they were back in Cairo, where Weeks became assistant professor of anthropology and Egyptology at the American University. The next year he became Field Director of Chicago House, a research center the University of Chicago runs in Luxor. The Weeks family—with two-year-old Christopher and six-month old Emily—moved into the research complex for a stay of four years. They lived happily amidst the thousands of ancient tombs and temples in the area—the Theban Necropolis, or burial ground, across the Nile from the ruins of the ancient Egyptian capital city of Thebes.

During the New Kingdom era of ancient Egypt, (about 1570 to 1070 B.C.) the rulers of Egypt were buried in tombs cut into the cliffs of the Valley of Kings, which stretches deep into the Western Desert. This important archeological area has been described and explored by innumerable travelers and scholars through the centuries. Napoleon Bonaparte sent a military expedition to Egypt in 1798 and scholars accompanying the campaign prepared some of the earliest maps of the Theban Necropolis. But these maps and those prepared by later visitors were all "sketchy, incomplete and inaccurate" and thousands of tombs were unexplored; others were entered, and perhaps plundered, but then lost.

Weeks believed it was essential to create a complete and detailed atlas of the region; showing the tombs, monuments, and temples in the immediate area of Thebes and Luxor, the palaces, settlements, and other structures on the desert hills nearby, and the thousands of tombs cut into the limestone cliffs in the Valley of the Kings. Maps would help archeologists and historians to locate and study the monuments. They also would help preservationists check the condition of the monuments, and make plans to protect them—from theft, vandalism, floods, new construction, invasion for irrigation and agriculture, and unrestricted tourism. In the face of rapid deterioration, Weeks believed the project had become urgent and decided he would have to take it on.

THE THEBAN MAPPING PROJECT

In 1976 Weeks and his family returned to the United States, and he became associate professor of Egyptian Archeology at the University of California, Berkeley, but did not give up his plan to map the necropolis. After getting some funding, he established the Theban Mapping Project (TMP)—an effort to create an archeological database of Thebes, showing the topography of the Valley and the three-dimensional placement of each tomb within the rock hills. Many archeologists consider the Theban Mapping Project vital to the documenting of Egypt's archeological heritage and the most important recent work in the region as preservation planning will be based on it. In addition, the project will make the site electronically accessible throughout the world. All information will be computerized, and a planned CD-ROM will allow virtual visitors to "fly" into each tomb to study its architecture and contents, and the murals and carvings on its walls. The TMP website (*http://www.KV5.com*) offers an up-to-date status report, views of recent finds, the history of the project, and other information.

The TMP crew first set out to establish a grid network so that archeological features could be located. It was hard work, in temperatures up to 120° F (50° C) equipment was technologically advanced, but heavy to transport, including electronic distance measuring machines with their battery packs, a theodolite (a surveying instrument), and others, and water and bags of cement (to shore up and stabilize structures).

After creating the grid, the team needed aerial photographs (in Howard Carter's day, all measurements would have been made on the ground—a much slower process). After a number of efforts to shoot aerial photos from airplanes failed, Weeks thought of using hot-air balloons as platforms from which to get the needed photos. This creative idea was a great success, and the balloon viewings of the valley were even adopted by a company that began offering them as a new attraction for tourists.

In the team's next season, the goal was to focus on the Valley of Kings; to map it and draw plans and sections, and create three-dimensional drawings of its tombs. The tombs had been numbered by an earlier explorer, John Gardner Wilkinson, in 1827. Wilkinson painted red numbers above every visible tomb entrance, labeling them KV1 (standing for Kings' Valley Tomb number 1) through KV21. Some of these tombs had already been excavated: Giovanni Belzoni explored KV17, the tomb of Seti I, father of Ramesses II, in 1817. Later archeologists located and labeled tombs 22 through 62 (62 was identified as Tutankhamen's tomb by Howard Carter in 1922).

THE LOST TOMBS

By the beginning of the 1989 excavation season, the TMP team had been working for more than ten years, and had mapped the entire Valley of the Kings and the Valley of the Queens, and some nearby areas. But there were some mysteries remaining. A few old sketches or reports from early visitors referred to about a dozen tomb entrances that the TMP could not locate. Weeks decided to spend the season looking for these "lost tombs." A factor adding urgency to his plan was the Egyptian Antiquities Organization's plan to widen the roadway at the entrance to the Valley of Kings. Weeks remembered that some old maps and reports had shown a tomb labeled KV5 (one of the unlocated tombs) very close to the valley entrance and he was afraid roadway construction would damage the tomb—if it was there.

The British traveler James Burton had burrowed a short distance into the tomb in 1825; his notes and a sketch intrigued Weeks because they suggested an unusual design. Howard Carter had also entered the tomb, but saw little of interest and then used its entrance-way as a dumping ground for ten feet of stone and dirt he cleared away from other nearby excavations. After that, the entrance of the tomb was covered over and forgotten.

The TMP team tried using geophysical devices—such as radar and magnetometry, or measuring variations in the earth's magnetic field—to locate the entrance of the tomb. In the end they relied on "old-fashioned archeological excavation: digging with a pick and shovel," and information from a number of sources including the diaries of nineteenth-century travelers, and the text of an ancient papyrus now in a museum in Turin, Italy. The papyrus text told of the 1150 B.C. trial of a thief who confessed under torture to robbing the tomb of Ramesses II, and another tomb "across the path"—perhaps KV5, which we now know to be 100 feet (30m) away.

THE TOMB OF A KING'S SONS

After about ten days of digging, Weeks and his workers uncovered the doorway of KV5—ten feet (3m) below the surface, behind the stalls of souvenir and postcard vendors that lined the approach road. They cleared the doorway, made a path into the debris-filled first chamber, and Weeks and two project workers crawled in. The name Ramesses II appeared in hieroglyphics on the doorway; there were traces of dec-oration on every wall they could see. Weeks reported "to us, the tomb looked promising"

Weeks and his workers spent the excavation seasons of the next five years in partially clearing the first two chambers, which were packed nearly to ceiling level with dirt and rocks washed in by floods, and briefly exploring a third chamber. Mixed in with the rubble were thousands of fragments and broken objects; jewelry, furniture, bones, grave goods, offerings. In the first two chambers, elaborate wall carvings referred to Ramesses II, and inscriptions and drawings showed the ruler presenting two of his sons to the gods. (Ramesses is said to have had 52 sons, and as many as 162 children, with 8 wives and an unknown number of concubines during his 67-year reign, from 1279 B.C. to 1212 B.C.). These led the excavators to believe that the tomb

This is the mummy of Ramesses II who was once the most powerful ruler of Egypt. He is said to have had at least 12 wives and more than 100 children.

was the burial place of his sons. The third chamber was a vast hall, sixty feet (18m) square, with sixteen massive stone pillars and, at the end the room, traces of an almost buried doorway.

Finally, in February 1995, Weeks decided to open that doorway, expecting to find nothing more than a "small number of small chambers that led nowhere." With one of his chief Egyptian workmen and an archeology graduate student, he struggled through the rubble, each one holding a flashlight. They crawled through a chamber beyond the doorway, through three more tiny rooms, a narrow tunnel, and into a long corridor, its walls punctuated by doorways. At the end of the corridor, inside a wall niche, they found the standing figure of Osiris, god of the Afterlife. It was carved out of rock, and its face was missing. Corridors on each side of the statue led into more chambers. Stairs led to more rooms below. Wall reliefs showed Isis and Osiris, the ibis-headed god Thoth, Anubis, the jackal-headed god of the dead, and other figures.

KV5

Now fully aware that KV5 was not merely another small tomb, Weeks calculated in his head and realized there were at least sixty-five chambers in the tomb—more than in any other. Weeks wrote in *The Lost Tomb*,

> *All at once I was overcome by a strange feeling, as we sat sixty meters (198-feet) underground, in utter silence, our light focused on a statue of the god of the Afterlife. Here, in the tomb of the great royal sons, in my imagination I could see the ancient funerals that took place three thousand years ago. I could hear ancient priests chanting prayers and shaking tambourines; I could feel the floor shake as great sarcophagi were dragged down the corridor; I could smell incense . . . as the funeral procession moved slowly past. For an instant, I felt transported back in time: it was 1275 BCE, and this was ancient Thebes.*

KV5 was unlike any tomb seen before. The largest tombs in the Valley have 10 or 15 rooms. KV5 is now thought to have more than

150. Most tombs consist of a string of chambers and corridors, leading to a burial chamber. KV5 follows a T shape, with side chambers and descending passageways, or as Weeks describes it, "like an octopus, with a body surrounded by tentacles." Nowhere else in Egypt has a multiple burial of a ruler's children been found. At KV5, at least four sons of Ramesses II are entombed, and perhaps many more.

The discovery of the largest rock-cut tomb ever found in Egypt was announced in June 1995, and drew attention throughout the world. The *New York Times* featured a page one story; *Time* magazine published a long feature article, the *Daily Mail* of London used the headline: "Pharaoh's 50 Sons in Mummy of All Tombs," for its article describing the find.

The exploration of KV5 is expected to reveal much about the New Kingdom period in Egypt, and there are many questions remaining to be answered about the tomb itself—including the purpose of its many chambers. Weeks has uncovered a human skeleton and four skulls, some of which may be from the disturbed mummies of the royal sons. He hopes to find the actual burial chambers, and uncover sarcophagi, funerary offerings, mummies, walls of hieroglyphics with much information, and perhaps even a treasure-filled chamber.

From the bone fragments, and if any mummified remains of the royal princes are found, DNA testing may yield more information about the royal families of the New Kingdom. However, some scientists question the accuracy of DNA tests on mummified remains. Weeks is more confident about getting useful information from a thorough study of the bones, teeth, and facial structure of the skulls.

KV5 is being excavated and documented carefully, by a professional team following rigorous archeological standards. It is sure to be an invaluable resource for study of ancient Egypt. There is still field work to be done. Susan Weeks is copying the wall reliefs for a reconstruction of the tomb decorations, and directing pottery analysis. Photographic surveys are underway. A topographer is generating maps and plans on a computer. And engineering work is being done to stabilize and protect the tomb.

Kent and Susan Weeks study drawings on the walls of KV5. Through his excavations, Weeks hopes to discover why this massive mausoleum was built more than 3,000 years ago. He also wants to learn the purpose of the many rooms in the tomb.

Kent Weeks says that he believes KV5 will be the "best-documented and best-protected tomb in the Valley of the Kings and its former occupants, the sons of Ramesses II, will have given us more information about their lives and their society than we have today." But some parts of the tomb will be left unexcavated, as a resource for future archeologists, with new techniques and new approaches, and their new sets of questions.

Weeks is continuing with work on KV5; and also with the Theban Mapping Project. In a *New Yorker* interview he promised that "having found the tomb, we've got an obligation to leave it in a good, stable, safe condition. . . . And we have an obligation to publish." Mortimer Wheeler would have been happy to have heard that.

Chapter 8
WHAT IS NEXT?

oday archeology is a sophisticated science; using knowledge and techniques from many related fields, with the goal of understanding the how, what, and why of human behavior on the basis of physical remains. Today's archeologists look at everything that can be unearthed or discovered, all the traces of human life: the homes, hearths, graves, temples and monuments, the tools, the drawings and pottery, the fields, the garbage pits, and anything else that bears the shadow of human life.

Researchers now have an array of new technologies. They use remote sensing devices to detect buried structures, satellite space imaging, ground penetrating radar and other means of geophysical prospection, computer-aided analysis of data and creation of maps, and DNA research to identify family relationships and perhaps provide information about human origins.

Archeological pioneers are working in many new areas:

- Underwater archeology is opening new areas of research. Pioneered by Jacques Cousteau's invention of the aqualung in 1943, archeologists can now excavate the seabed, studying thousands of shipwrecks from every era, adding to our knowledge of the history of shipbuilding and ancient trade routes.

Underwater archeology is an exciting new field. Here, scuba divers investigate a shipwreck in the Bahamas.

- Urban archeologists study how cities developed, and the spread of urbanization. The recent excavation of an eighteenth-century cemetery for people from Africa or African descent in New York City, shows how archeology expands the historical record, particularly in the case of overlooked segments of society.

This archeological site is in New York City. Workers sort through discoveries at the only known burial ground for Africans or people of African descent before the American Revolution.

This skeleton was found at the burial ground site in New York City.

- Salvage archeology is aimed at preserving threatened sites, such as at Abu Simbel.
- Industrial archeology investigates manufacturing and industries of the past. At Bethlehem Steel in Pennsylvania, a National Museum of Industrial History is under construction, to preserve and exhibit the now abandoned methods of iron and steel manufacturing.
- Landscape archeology studies human societies in their environmental settings over time, observing how they responded to changes in the landscape and their impact on the environment.

There are many other subfields, ranging from archeoastronomy to zooarcheology. And even in fields as long-established as biblical archeology, Egyptology, Mesoamerican archeology, and others, discoveries and interpretations continue to appear at an astounding rate, to provide answers to old questions and, sometimes, to ask new ones.

The pioneering aspect of archeology remains as true today as in the days of Belzoni and Howard Carter. Today's scientific frontier is the past—the history of humankind. This is a challenging, important frontier, with many unexplored areas and mysteries, and much fresh digging to be done.

GLOSSARY

absolute dating—assigning a specific time to a relic (see *relative dating*).

antiquity—a relic or monument from ancient times; coins, statues, or other material.

archeology—the study of ancient things. The study of the social and cultural past through material remains, with the aim of reconstructing the history of human beings. A science concerned with reconstructing and understanding human behavior on the basis of the material remains left by our prehistoric and historic forebears.

artifacts—manufactured, human-made objects from an earlier time, such as arrowheads, tools, pottery, sculpture.

chronology—a system of arranging events in the order in which they occurred; a list of dates in the order of occurrence.

cuneiform—a form of writing, derived from Latin words meaning "wedge-shaped." Invented in the Mesopotamian region about the end of the fourth millennium B.C. and used until around 100 A.D. It began as stylized pictures of objects drawn on clay with a reed stylus, which made wedge-shaped impressions.

Egyptologist—an archeologist who specializes in the study of ancient Egypt.

excavation—a dig, a planned systematic effort to investigate an ancient site, to gain information about human behavior in the past. The process of excavation is destructive, and is therefore now used selectively, when necessary, to allow the study of archeological records.

grid—a pattern of squares that covers the excavation site. Excavation is carried out within each square.

hieroglyphics—from Greek words meaning "sacred carving." Used to describe the pictographic writing of ancient Egypt, from the end of the fourth millennium B.C. to the fourth century A.D. Individual signs (hieroglyphs) are carved or painted on stone, wood, or plaster. A picture-based writing system in which each sign represents an object.

industrial archeology—the study of past industrial methods; especially from the earliest days of the industrial revolution.

mound—an elevated area of earth. Natural mounds are formed by regular strata deposited by natural means; artificial mounds may have been built as fortifications, as ceremonial mounds, as platforms for buildings, or burial sites.

prehistory—the study of humankind in the period before writing.

relative dating—Determining the chronological sequence of relics—which are the oldest, the newest—without reference to a fixed time scale (see *absolute dating*).

reliefs—figures and shapes carved onto a flat surface.

salvage archeology—excavations aimed at preserving, saving, or studying a site before it is lost or destroyed by construction projects or other hazards.

sarcophagus—a stone coffin.

site—an area of archeological excavation and study, a cluster of relics and archeological features.

strata—the different levels or layers of deposits in soil.

stratigraphy—the study of the strata, or layers, of physical deposits laid one on top of another. The lowest layers are the oldest.

tell—a mound formed from the build-up of material as a result of the occupation by people.

topography—the study of the natural and human-created features of the landscape.

SELECTED BIBLIOGRAPHY

Chapter 1
LOOKING INTO THE PAST

Daniel, Glyn. *A Hundred and Fifty Years of Archaeology*. Cambridge: Harvard University Press, 1975.

Fagan, Brian M., ed. *The Oxford Companion to Archaeology*. New York: Oxford University Press, 1996.

Magnusson, Magnus. *Introducing Archaeology*. London: The Bodley Head, 1972.

Chapter 2
GIOVANNI BELZONI

Belzoni, Giovanni. *Narrative of the Operations and Recent Discoveries within the Pyramids, Temples, Tombs, and Excavations, in Egypt and Nubia*. London: John Murray, 1820.

Norman, Bruce. *Footsteps: Nine Archaeological Journeys of Romance and Discovery*. Topsfield, Mass.: Salem House, 1988.

Wilkins, Frances. *Six Great Archaeologists: Belzoni, Layard, Schliemann, Evans, Carter, Thompson*. London: Hamish Hamilton, 1961.

Chapter 3
HOWARD CARTER AND LORD CARNARVON

Carter, Howard, and A. C. Mace. *The Discovery of the Tomb of Tutankhamen*. New York: Dover Publications, 1977.

Desroches-Noblecourt, Christiane. *Tutankhamen*. Boston: New York Graphic Society, 1963.

Fagan, Brian, M., ed. *Eyewitness to Discovery*. New York: Oxford University Press, 1996.

Chapter 4
HIRAM BINGHAM

Bingham, Hiram. *Lost City of the Incas*. New York: Atheneum, 1975.

Fagan, Brian, M., ed. *Eyewitness to Discovery*. New York: Oxford University Press, 1996.

Norman, James. *The Riddle of the Incas*. New York: Hawthorn Books, 1968.

Chapter 5
MORTIMER WHEELER

Hawkes, Jacquetta. *Adventurer in Archaeology: The Biography of Sir Mortimer Wheeler*. New York: St. Martin's Press, 1982

Wheeler, Mortimer. *Still Digging*. New York: E. P. Dutton & Co., Inc. 1955.

_____. *Archaeology from the Earth*. New York: Oxford University Press, 1954.

Chapter 6
GERTRUDE BELL AND KATHLEEN KENYON

Fagan, Brian M., ed. *Eyewitness to Discovery*. New York: Oxford University Press, 1996.

Hawkes, Jacquetta. *Adventurer in Archaeology, The Biography of Sir Mortimer Wheeler*. New York: St. Martin's Press, 1982.

Kenyon, Kathleen. *Digging Up Jericho*. New York: Frederick A. Praeger, 1957.

Wallach, Janet. *Desert Queen*. New York: Nan Talese/Doubleday, 1996.

Chapter 7
KENT R. WEEKS

Lemonick, Michael D. "Secrets of the Lost Tomb." *Time*, May 29, 1995, pp. 49-54.

Preston, Douglas. "All the King's Sons." Annals of Archeology. *New Yorker*, January 22, 1996, pp. 44-59.

"Valley of the Kings Megatomb." *Archaeology*, July/August 1995, pp. 18-19.

Weeks, Kent R., Ph.D. *The Lost Tomb: In 1995, an American Egyptologist Discovered the Burial Site of the Sons of Ramesses II. This Is His Incredible Story of KV5 and Its Excavation*. New York: William Morrow and Co., Inc., 1998.

Wilford, John Noble. "Tomb of Ramses II's Many Sons Is Found in Egypt." *New York Times*, May 1995.

FOR MORE INFORMATION

BOOKS

Ceram, C. W. *Gods, Graves, and Scholars: The Story of Archaeology.* New York: Alfred Knopf, 1952. A classic and readable work, for general readers.

Fagan, Brian M., Ed. *Eyewitness to Discovery: First-Person Accounts of More Than Fifty of the World's Greatest Archaeological Discoveries.* New York: Oxford University Press, 1996. A celebration of archeological discoveries, and the men and women who made them.

_____. *The Oxford Companion to Archaeology.* New York: Oxford University Press, 1996. A useful reference work.

Magnusson, Magnus. *Introducing Archaeology.* London: The Bodley Head, 1972. A lively introduction to the subject.

Silverberg, Robert. *Great Adventures in Archaeology.* Lincoln and London: University of Nebraska Press, 1964. Ten archeologists tell the stories of their explorations. An entertaining anthology.

Wade, Nicholas, ed. *The Science Times Book of Archaeology.* New York: The Lyons Press, 1999. The stories of important archeological discoveries, as reported in the *New York Times*.

INTERNET RESOURCES

The American Museum of Natural History
http://www.amnh.org
Exhibits and information about prehistoric and historic life.

Ancient Sites
http://www.AncientSites.com
Re-creations of ancient cities, with historical quizzes, tours, and games, for amusement and information.

The Ancient World Web
http://www.julen.net/ancient/
An annotated index of more than 900 sites dealing with archeology.

Archnet
http://archnet.uconn.edu
A WWW virtual library for archeology.

***Archaeology* Magazine**
http://www.archaeology.org
The website of an attractive monthly magazine of archeological news.

***National Geographic* Magazine**
http://www.nationalgeographic.com
The website of the monthly magazine.

INDEX

ABOUT THE AUTHORS

Lorna Greenberg and Margot F. Horwitz share an interest in past civilizations and in the personal stories of those who have led the way in exploring them.

Lorna Greenberg is a children's book editor and writer. Her works include a project on early civilizations and *AIDS: How It Works in the Body*, which was selected for a Science Books and Films list of Best Children's Science Books. She lives in New York.

Margot Horwitz is a writer and former public-relations advisor for non-profit organizations. Her earlier books include *A Female Focus: Great Women Photographers* and *Claudia "Lady Bird" Taylor Johnson*, a biography of the former first lady. She lives in Pennsylvania.